ALSO BY CHARLES FRIED

Minorities: Community and Identity (editor)

Contract as Promise: A Theory of Contractual Obligation

Right and Wrong

Medical Experimentation: Personal Integrity and Social Policy

An Anatomy of Values

ORDER *and* LAW

*Arguing
the Reagan Revolution
—A Firsthand Account*

Charles Fried

SOLICITOR GENERAL, REAGAN ADMINISTRATION
1985–1989

SIMON & SCHUSTER
New York   London   Toronto   Sydney   Tokyo   Singapore

Simon & Schuster
Simon & Schuster Building
Rockefeller Center
1230 Avenue of the Americas
New York, New York 10020

Designed by Carla Weise/Levavi & Levavi
Manufactured in the United States of America

1   3   5   7   9   10   8   6   4   2

Library of Congress Cataloging-in-Publication Data

Fried, Charles, date.
Order and law : arguing the Reagan revolution : a firsthand
account / Charles Fried.
p.   cm.
Includes bibliographical references and index.
1. Political questions and judicial power—United States.
2. Courts—United States.   3. United States—Politics and
government—1981–   4. Conservatism—United States.
5. Reagan, Ronald.   6. Fried, Charles, date   I. Title.
KF8700.F75   1991
347.73′1—dc20
[347.3071]   91-2114
CIP

ISBN 0-671-72575-0

TO THE MEMORY OF MY MOTHER

CONTENTS

Preface   11

Introduction
The Reagan Revolution and the Law   13

Chapter 1
Setting the Scene   23

Chapter 2
Interpretation   55

Chapter 3
Privacy   71

Chapter 4
Race   89

Chapter 5
Powers   132

Chapter 6
Loyalty   172

Notes   207

Index   246

PREFACE

The events and controversies I describe in this book take on a different aspect as they recede. Many things have happened to change how the world looks—none more important to me than the fall of communism in my native Czechoslovakia in the remarkable "November Days" of 1989. I have not tried to take account of the continuing development of the issues I discuss. None of these issues will soon come to rest. So if I had done that, I might not have written this book at all. The perspective I take up here is the one I had more or less as I left office.

Many people commented on drafts of all or part of this book: Donald Ayer, Derrick Bell, Sissela Bok, Michael Boudin, Stephen Breyer, Terry Fisher, Gregory Fried, Philip Heymann, Judith Hope, Randall Kennedy, Carolyn Kuhl, Harvey Mansfield, Martha Minow, Glenn Nager, John Noonan, Richard Parker, Massimo Piatelli-Palmarini, David Rosenberg, Kenneth Starr, Cass Sunstein, Richard Taranto, James Thompson, David Wilkins, and the members of the Society for Ethical and Legal Philosophy. It is more than usually necessary to absolve them of all blame for the judgments and errors in the final product. I thank my research assistants, Daniel Bromberg, Mark Filip,

Thomas Perrelli, Edward Reitler, Eric Scheuermann, and Brian Tamanaha. Robert Barnett encouraged me at every stage of this undertaking. Alice Mayhew was an extraordinary and relentless editor.

Cambridge, October 1990

INTRODUCTION: THE REAGAN REVOLUTION AND THE LAW

The state is that great fictitious entity by which everyone seeks to live at the expense of everyone else.[1]

*F*rom 1985 to 1989 I was the Reagan administration's Solicitor General. My friends in the left-liberal establishment despised Ronald Reagan as ill-educated, comically simple-minded, and dangerously stubborn about the few things he believed strongly. I liked him from the start. Something about being a Czech Jew—driven out of a prosperous, bourgeois country first by one total vision of government and then by another—made me share Reagan's gut-level dislike for the pretensions of government in general. I also sensed a deep and fundamental decency about Ronald Reagan. He was an old man. He knew what he believed. He was comfortable in his skin. In this he was the antithesis of Richard Nixon, who had always struck me as so eerily devious and inhuman that he should not be trusted with leadership. From the start I liked Ronald Reagan's simple but understandable version of principles I believed in too.

"What does the Solicitor General do?" sounds like a Trivial Pursuit question, yet the Solicitor General has always been a crucial member of the President's establishment. In this century two Chief Justices and several Associate Justices have had the job. The office was created in the Judiciary Act of 1870: "There shall be an officer, learned in the law, to assist the Attorney General." Because of the massive shift of authority to the national government during the Civil War and Reconstruction, the Attorney General gradually became not just the legal adviser to the President[2] but the administrative head of a vast establishment that today includes the FBI, the Immigration Service, the Border Patrol, the Marshall Service, the Bureau of Prisons—in all some seventy thousand persons. But the Solicitor General's job has hardly changed since 1870. He still goes to the Supreme Court in morning coat and striped trousers as the principal spokesman there of the government. It is his job to approve what the government will say in any appellate court in the country. His staff is small (about twenty lawyers), and he takes personal, not just bureaucratic, responsibility for every decision, every brief he signs. In a real sense the Solicitor General is responsible for the government's legal theories, its legal philosophy. And legal philosophy was at the heart of the Reagan Revolution.

The Reagan Revolution challenged a set of overlapping, even contradictory orthodoxies, some going back to the New Deal, others the result of the civil-rights movement, the Vietnam protests, and the scandal of Watergate. From the New Deal days came an exaggerated faith in bureaucracy and government expertise; a distaste for capitalism and free enterprise and a fondness for government redistribution of wealth; a belief in democratic socialism as a more humane, more modern form of economic organization. Though much of the energy had gone out of this old-style progressivism, the Vietnam War left quite a different legacy: a belief in the inevitable decline of American influence and prestige; a conviction that military power is irrelevant and useless; a sense that the history of American dealings with other countries, as with our own minorities and with our own poor people, was so far tainted that the prosperous had not earned their prosperity and that the poor were the victims of everyone else (as if the way we had treated the American Indian typified our treatment of everything and everyone—including one another). There was a nagging doubt that by punishing criminals we just compounded our crimes against those who were less offenders than victims. And an ideological environmental movement[3] gave us the ultimate victim in mother nature herself, with man as the ultimate oppressor.

Watergate focused this cynicism and self-hatred. What we should have learned from that sordid episode is that the exercise of authority is often accompanied by hypocrisy and machinations of every kind. We should have understood that any enduring and powerful regime must face the challenge of carrying on practical politics while keeping such departures within tolerable limits. Instead Watergate was seen as a confirmation that those who govern must not be trusted with the means or discretion of governing effectively. We were told that as a nation we had lost the right—if we had ever had it—to be governed effectively and to act effectively in the world. Our whole society—our government and all our major public and private institutions—must be put on probation, with judges, public-interest lawyers, journalists, and adversary politicians acting as our probation officers. All established and successful "elite" institutions were regarded as suspect—businesses, universities, professions, or governments. The presidency was seen as a particularly dangerous elite that had to be hemmed in by Congress, by a permanent bureaucracy, and by legal procedures and rules of all sorts.

Above all, the left-liberal orthodoxies embraced the premise that the federal judiciary should be the engine for realizing their values. To fulfill its proper role, the judiciary must act as guarantor of the progressive program, making good this guarantee by manipulating rules and remedies at every level, and if need be by creating new constitutional rights. Ways of interpreting authoritative texts—precedents, laws, the Constitution—must be appropriately supple and expansive.[4] Lawsuits must be recast so they would not just be disputes between individuals over their particular grievances but political struggles in which judges could reorder whole institutions and change the fundamental nature of society. Rules of procedure, standing, and representation must allow for the role of progressive-minded lawyers and legal organizations as the moving parties of these radical social changes.[5]

The Reagan Revolution wanted a more confident society and a less intrusive government. The campaign was fought on two fronts. First, tax reduction was supposed to starve politicians of the resources with which they would regulate the economy, pursue their favorite projects, redistribute wealth, and reward clients who kept them in office. The other front was the legal front.

That battle was fought in the courts, which had for years been complicit in the aggrandizement of government. In many respects the courts themselves had become major bureaucratic actors, enthusiastically, self-consciously enlisting in the movement to substitute the judgments and values of the nonproductive sector of society—lawyers, judges, bureaucrats, politicians—for the self-determination of the entrepreneurs and workers who create wealth. Egged on by aggressive litigators, the legal professoriate, and the liberal press, the courts had become a principal engine for redistributing wealth and shackling the energies and enterprise of the productive sector.

The Solicitor General stood at the center of the project of returning the courts to the position of neutral and modest arbiters between man and man, deciding cases according to known rules (and if sometimes with a certain wooden literalness, no harm in that). He was the David Stockman of the legal agenda.

The tenets of the Reagan Revolution were clear: courts should be more disciplined, less adventurous and political in interpreting the law, especially the law of the Constitution; the President must be allowed a strong hand in governing the nation and providing leadership; justice and racial equality could be—and so should be—achieved without twisting legal principles, and without distorting the system of opportunity and reward for merit on which the morale of a free-enterprise system depends.

These convictions had to come to terms with other, conflicting realities. First of all, as Tocqueville had said a long time ago, our Constitution and traditions make law and the courts the focus of controversies that in other societies are the subjects of ordinary politics—perhaps to the detriment of the quality of our politics and politicians. And any approach to the role of law and the courts had to take account of the Himalayan fact that it was the Supreme Court in *Brown* v. *Board*—not the ordinary political system—that had taken the largest step since Reconstruction in dismantling legalized racism and apartheid in this country. It was the courts and the Supreme Court that had moved to civilize the way local police departments dealt with criminal suspects—particularly the poor and the ignorant. And it was the courts and the Supreme Court that had made our system of individual liberty a model for the whole world. It would have been not just Quixotic but anticonstitutional and thus lawless to seek a wholesale reversal of that tradition.

So, inevitably, there were contradictions and cross-currents in the heart of the revolution. How does the impulse to reduce the intrusion of government into people's lives work with the abortion issue? The move to overturn *Roe* v. *Wade* was seen by some as a push to allow a violent intrusion into the most private aspect of our private lives. How does the conservative ideal of limited government mesh with the campaign for greater presidential autonomy? We saw that push in our attack on the Independent Counsel law, a law some said did no more than subject the President and his men to the rule of law. Does the insistence that constitutional equality is a principle that applies to individuals, not to groups, betray indifference to the history and the present reality of racial injustice?

Each view came with a constituency—more or less disinterested—and each constituency had its champions in the administration. The Reagan majority was notoriously a coalition of businesspeople who were interested in lower taxes and less government spending; free-market libertarians; neoconservatives who were most interested in an assertive anticommunist foreign policy; social conservatives who were concerned to see the political and social culture take on a texture that they associated (probably somewhat romantically and inaccurately) with the style of the pre-JFK era; the religious right, which had a quite explicit and demanding agenda that included severely restricting the availability of abortions, allowing spoken prayer in the public schools, and suppressing anything (like a tolerance of pornography) that smacked of liberal permissiveness; and finally what might be called habitual or professional Republicans, who instinctively may have been a bit more conservative than the average Democrat but whose main allegiance was to the party. It is striking that this last group, which in other times would have been the center of any Republican administration, was often relegated to the fringes of the Reagan administration. Party loyalty counted for comparatively little and was rewarded rather meagerly compared with philosophical commitment. Former Democrats were welcomed as Coriolanus come among the Volscians; this was true not only of Jeane Kirkpatrick or Bill Bennett, but of Ronald Reagan himself.

The first major brief I filed as Acting Solicitor General argued that the Supreme Court should over-rule *Roe* v. *Wade.* After I had left office and returned to Harvard, the Bush administration called me back to make the same argument in the *Webster* case.[6] Abortion seemed to be a principal preoccupation of my tenure, but for me *Roe* was just a symptom of a mistaken approach to judging, an approach that confused and threatened the ideal of the rule of law. The struggle against quotas and racial preferences, imposed in the name of affirmative action, was another persistent theme of my work. But here too there was a deeper worry. I was concerned about government taking over too many of the prerogatives that in a healthy, liberal society properly belong to individuals and to private institutions. And I was worried as well about courts imposing a collectivist conception of equality that had no warrant in the Constitution, the civil-rights laws, or our traditions as a society. Finally, I was involved in some dramatic battles about the separation of powers: Gramm-Rudman,[7] the Independent Counsel,[8] the sentencing guidelines.[9] In part I was doing my job as an advocate for the President in defending his prerogatives against encroachments by Congress. But the deeper theme was an orderly, coherent conception of government, where powers and responsibility are assigned in a way that the ordinary citizen can under-stand. This too is an aspect of the rule of law.

The public-policy questions I presented to the

Supreme Court came embedded in an overall vision for the country, a critique of where we had been and where we should be going. But attitudes on such a wide array of subjects are hardly a function of pure reason, of abstract thought alone—although the Reagan presidency was accompanied by more abstract theorizing than is usual in American politics. (This is what made quite apt Ronald Reagan's frequent comparisons of himself to Franklin Roosevelt—although they elicited grimaces of rage or smirks of derision from those who considered themselves the true heirs of the FDR legacy.) Such large movements are also a function of persons and of personality: the President's first of all, but of all the principal actors and advisers who tried to make the revolution.

1

SETTING THE SCENE

*Here is an unfailing rule: a prince who is
not himself wise cannot be well advised.*

—MACHIAVELLI, *The Prince*

On the Fringe

The first time I argued to a court was to the Supreme
Court in 1985. I had been a law teacher at Harvard
ever since finishing a Supreme Court clerkship in
1961. I had not been active in politics or done
anything much besides teaching and writing. In the
spring of 1980 I had mentioned to a Harvard colleague who was working for candidate Ronald Reagan that I would like to become involved in the
campaign. I had to admit that I was the most general
of generalists. I had written some short journalistic

pieces on public issues. But my academic subjects were moral and social philosophy and contract law, so I was hardly an obvious resource to a political campaign. Worse for me: I knew nothing about Washington and Republican politics, had barely heard of the Heritage Foundation, and knew none of the main personalities.

It was with some embarrassment that I faced the questions put to me by Darrell Trent, the chief issues man in the campaign: what do you know, what can you do? He assigned me to the task force on regulatory reform, since I was committed to deregulation both as a scholar and as a publicist.[1] My essay for that task force was made up largely of impressions and intuitions: our regulatory process had become too entangled with legalisms; lawyers, judges, and bureaucrats had too large a role in it. Mine was a casual piece of work, but it turned out some of my major battles—with the Labor Board and the Department of Labor, with the Federal Reserve Board, and with my own staff—and some of my biggest cases[2] bore on those intuitions.

The election of 1980 was exhilarating. And now I wanted to become part of the new administration. I was as naïve going about this as when I first tried to become involved in the campaign. I thought that I could be choosy, that good offers would come to me more or less on their own. A well-connected friend had advised me that I should do nothing and let them come to me, that sending my résumé to the transition officials (who were sorting through thousands of résumés) would work against me. Through November, December, and January hordes of office-seekers descended, just as Henry Adams described in his novel

Democracy, or as Walt Whitman experienced it after the election of 1864: "Tides of office seekers, profiteers, and promoters, voyeurs, zealots, do-gooders, quacks, religious enthusiasts, prostitutes, swindlers, scamperers from ruined reputations . . . [driving] up the price of food and drink"[3]—and, I would add, the price of real estate. By early February, when I should have realized it was already too late for the first round, a former student—who did know his way around and was working those first chaotic months in the White House with a focused gaze on a particular Assistant Secretary's slot—said he would like to help. I should send him my résumé. I expressed it to him—three times. Finally, in late February 1981, Trent (now installed as Deputy Secretary of Transportation) personally took me around to his friends in the White House. In a crowded West Wing passageway, I ran into my former student. He greeted me warmly. What was I doing here? Really? I should have turned to him for help. Perhaps even now it was not too late. I should send him my résumé.

There was a lot of talk during that White House tour, but in the end what I wanted I could not have, and what I could have I did not want. I learned what should have been obvious—that the White House personnel office is not interested in providing personal fulfillment for individual office-seekers. There are a lot of slots to be filled, and warm bodies with plausible credentials to fill them. The experienced office-seeker homes in on a specific job and persuades personnel that he solves their problems by filling it. Or else he accepts whatever is offered and then plans how to continue his climb from base camp.

Trent was a good and persistent friend. He kept in

touch and asked me to help him with some of his regulatory issues: Japanese automobile imports, deregulating international airline fares and maritime freight. In the summer of 1982 he suggested me to David Stockman as the chief of the agency within the Office of Management and Budget that tried to enforce regulatory reform on the Executive Branch bureaucracies. In the course of a day's meetings in the White House I (and probably others) realized that I did not know a lot about how this particular bureaucracy worked. The job went to an able lawyer-economist, whom Stockman probably had had in mind from the start. But during this visit I made friends with some of the policy people in the White House: Edwin Harper, who would soon replace Martin Anderson as Assistant to the President for Policy Development, and Michael Horowitz, Stockman's counsel, a White House man-of-all-work and one of the most creative, outspoken, abrasive, and mercurial figures of the first Reagan administration.[4]

In June 1982 Horowitz persuaded Harper to make me head of an informal White House working group on employment discrimination. The other members were Civil Rights chief Brad Reynolds and Clarence Thomas, the Chairman of the Equal Employment Opportunity Commission and one of the few blacks in the administration. It became clear that this was a project Horowitz had cooked up to push the President to rescind the Executive Order setting up a special bureaucracy to make businesses working with the government meet goals and timetables for minority employment.[5] Because of the way it had been administered in the past, the Executive Order was seen as a symbol of the old racial politics, and rescinding it would show that Reagan was willing to act on his strongly stated dislike for quotas and government-imposed race preferences. Yet the President's chief advisers were reluctant just now to do anything that would be seen as dramatically hostile to civil rights. The administration had stuck its neck way out and got its head chopped off by urging the Supreme Court in the *Bob Jones* case[6] to allow a college with a bizarre rule against interracial dating to keep its tax exemption. The working group was intended to overcome this reluctance, which had settled in after *Bob Jones*. I wrote a strong brief for getting the government out of the general business of imposing quotas and preferences, except as a last resort to bring proven discriminators into line. Reynolds and I had a sharp disagreement on that last point: he would not countenance preferences even in such cases. Clarence Thomas, who became one of my most important clients when I was Solicitor General, was willing to see stronger remedies in individual cases of proven discrimination.

I can still picture the chilling way Reynolds made his points: the cold stare, the tense, high-pitched, but quiet voice speaking between clenched teeth. In the end, we agreed to disagree. Harper showed my draft recommendations to Ed Meese, who was then Reagan's chief domestic-policy counselor. Meese and I had a brief conversation, and Harper asked a few questions. They were worried that businesses might be squeezed between lawsuits by blacks and women over unbalanced work forces and a new class of lawsuits by white males hurt by voluntary affirmative-action programs. They decided to hold off any decision about the Executive Order for a time. It is still in effect.

At about the same time, in the spring and summer of 1982, I was also advising Attorney General Smith's staff. They and the White House had become increasingly unhappy with the Solicitor General's office. There was muttering that Rex Lee, the Solicitor General, was not aggressive enough about "pushing the President's agenda" and too deferential to Congress, to the agencies, and to the bureaucracy. This grumbling came to me in the form of complaints about how the career lawyers in the Solicitor General's office had much more influence with Lee than did his political peers in the administration. The criticism was odd, since it was Lee who personally argued and won some of the administration's biggest early victories.[7] Matters had come to a head in the *Bob Jones* case. Lee had recused himself because of previous professional work for one of the parties, leaving the case to Lawrence Wallace, the senior career Deputy. Wallace resisted the project. When his arguments on the merits were dismissed, he turned to complex bureaucratic and procedural arguments. The episode drew attention to the fact that no one in the Solicitor General's office but the Solicitor General himself had been appointed by the administration. All the lawyers in that office were career civil servants. In most other major offices of government the principal deputy is also a political appointee. Had there been such a person in Wallace's place, there might even have been some small chance that the *Bob Jones* brief would never have been filed.

Attorney General Smith invited me to meet with him to discuss becoming the first noncareer Deputy Solicitor General; there were four career Deputies. Because it would have been awkward to move to

Washington just then and because I had no idea yet how strategic the Solicitor General's office was, I turned the job down. I did not come to my meeting with the Attorney General empty-handed: I urged Smith to appoint my Harvard colleague Paul Bator. Bator was a leading expert on federal jurisdiction and administrative law; he had the reputation of being quite conservative; he was not known as a Reagan partisan, and so the innovation would be less abruptly political; and he had signed a political advertisement citing candidate Reagan's distinguished record on judicial appointments as Governor of California, thus rebutting unfair charges that, as President, Reagan would destroy the federal judiciary. Smith's only worry was that Bator's lack of overt political affiliation would make him unacceptable to the White House. It was at that point that I unfurled a copy of the campaign ad. Bator was named Deputy and (at his insistence) Counselor to the Solicitor General. This title was to set him off from the career deputies. Rex Lee was not yet ready to brave the displeasure of his staff by displacing Wallace and making Bator principal deputy.

At first the Solicitor General's office resisted Bator as an alien presence, but his work soon proved him to be a man of brilliance, elegance, talent, and integrity. He argued and won a number of difficult and controversial cases and briefed others.[8] He also distinguished himself by eloquently opposing at least one truly harebrained project which was even more wrongheaded than *Bob Jones*. Federal District Judge Brevard Hand had ruled in favor of the constitutionality of state-mandated spoken prayers in Alabama public schools.[9] His opinion contained the remarkable suggestion that he, a district judge, might over-rule a long line of Supreme Court precedents.[10] And some in the Department were suggesting that the United States enter the case in the court of appeals in support of Judge Hand's decision. The Reagan agenda certainly included asking the Supreme Court to reconsider a number of its own precedents—sometimes with a fair measure of success.[11] But of course that is different from encouraging a lower federal court to disregard settled Supreme Court law. The proposal was being debated seriously enough that Attorney General Smith's Counselor, Ken Starr (who was one of the few political persons in the Department to oppose the *Bob Jones* caper), tele-phoned me at Harvard to ask my advice. My response was to describe the project as a kamikaze mission in which only the pilot would get killed.

In 1983 and 1984 my personal need to be in Cambridge lessened, while the squabbles caused by the extreme-left Critical Legal Studies Movement at the Harvard Law School had become increasingly disagreeable. Bator's leave of absence, which by Har-vard's rule may not exceed two years, was due to end.[12] By the summer of 1984 I had decided that, if I was ever going to take part in the administration, I had better speak up for the one position on which I had a pretty good claim. I called Bator and asked him to pass the word that I would like to replace him.

It took longer than I expected for my offer to be accepted. My appointment as Deputy Solicitor Gen-eral had to be approved by the White House, which meant by Ed Meese. Bill Smith was planning to resign, and Ed Meese expected to become Attorney General sometime early in the second presidential term—after an Independent Counsel gave his report on Meese's personal finances. Though I did not know it then, Meese was planning to give the Department a harder philosophical edge, and that meant major personnel changes. I guess now, from the grumbling that was heard about Lee in conservative quarters, that the original plan may have been to move Lee out and name Reynolds Solicitor General. It was clear, however, because of *Bob Jones* and other controversial stands he had taken as Civil Rights chief, that Reynolds stood little chance of getting the Senate to confirm him to that job. So another scheme was hatched. I would guess that Reynolds' failed nomination to be Associate Attorney General (the number-three post in the Department) shortly after Meese took over had been intended as a way station to his becoming the Deputy Attorney General. As Deputy, Reynolds would have almost the same status as the Attorney General, and thus would be in a position to try to give orders to the Solicitor General. Ken Cribb was coming over as the Attorney General's Counselor, bringing with him a cadre of eager, philosophically committed young assistants. I would also suppose that Meese and Cribb wanted to leave themselves free to make their own choices for the top slots in the Department once they got there. Nevertheless, by October 1984 my appointment was settled, and I began part-time work right away. On February 1, 1985, I began on a full-time basis.

Moving to the Center

Those first months were my happiest, most innocent time in Washington. Apart from the fun and novelty of working on briefs and arguing in the Supreme Court, the most exhilarating part of my work was chairing the Litigation Strategy Working Group. The group, made up of political deputies, tried to bring some philosophical coherence to the work of the Department's litigating divisions (Anti-Trust, Civil, Civil Rights, Criminal, Lands and Natural Resources, and Tax). Our sessions were more like seminars than meetings of government officials. It was a way for me to learn about the work of the Department and to develop my own ideas about subjects I had never thought about. The members of our group became my good friends, and remain so in spite of differences that inevitably arose after I became Solicitor General. Some of them later moved up to be heads of their divisions,[13] and Carolyn Kuhl, Deputy in the Civil Division, whom Meese had wanted to make head of Civil Rights if his plan to advance Reynolds had succeeded, became my Counselor for the first year I served as Solicitor General. The seniors of these Deputies were also unusually young. They paid attention to what came out of our group. They became my good friends too. Even Brad Reynolds, who was older than the others and seemed to have large numbers of unspecified, high-level duties within the administration, would join in our conversations.

In April 1985 Rex Lee told me that he was leaving at the end of the Supreme Court term, a date he then advanced to the end of May 1985. That left me, as Acting Solicitor General. A law teacher and the father of a large family, Lee needed to repair his finances after four years in office. I suspect that the lack of appreciation from the hard right and no encouragement by the new Attorney General hastened his departure. I had argued in the Supreme Court (or any court) only three times, and thus at first did not give any thought to succeeding Rex permanently. But I did feel that, having been head of the office, even on an acting basis, I would not want to be second again.

Right after I became Acting Solicitor General, the Supreme Court agreed to hear *Thornburgh* v. *American College of Obstetricians and Gynecologists*,[14] the first abortion case in two years, the first since the President's re-election, and the first for the Meese Justice Department. Abortion was a signal issue for the administration, joining the strong prolife sentiments of the President's religious-right, traditionalist constituency with the more professional sense (shared by a broad array of respected academic commentators[15]) that *Roe* v. *Wade* was an extreme example of judicial overreaching—a position with which I agreed. Some of the political people in the Department were eager to "stand up and be counted" on this hottest of issues. But the pressure on me to file a brief in the case was neither excessive nor improper. The divisions which would be heard on such issues—Civil, Civil Rights, and Legal Policy—all wrote recommendations in ordinary course. The most aggressive memo came from my friends Richard Willard and Carolyn Kuhl in Civil, who recommended that we urge outright reversal of *Roe*.

The career deputies on my staff were understandably anxious about this exercise. The last time they had had to endure an abortion brief was when Lee had entered the *Akron* case three years before.[16] There he had written an oddly ambiguous essay, which seemed to accept the premise of *Roe* but urged extreme deference to the legislature in applying it.

When Lee rose to argue, Justice Blackmun, *Roe*'s author, waved the brief in his face and, after asking if Lee had written it, demanded to know if he was asking that *Roe* be overruled ("Not at this time, Your Honor") and, if not, if he was then asking that *Marbury* v. *Madison* be overruled. From this episode the career staff drew the conclusion that, for the sake of the many other cases we had before the Court, we had better stay out of abortion cases altogether. They hoped that I, as their acting chief, would stand up to the pressure and just decline to enter.

In meetings with Willard, Kuhl, Cooper, and Reynolds I raised my staff's arguments. This only rekindled the feeling that the career staff in the Solicitor General's office were more interested in protecting their "special relationship to the Court" than in arguing their "client's" position. It was clear to me that, as Acting Solicitor General, I could not succeed in heading off an anti-*Roe* brief, even if I had been convinced that that was the right thing to do. I would simply be overruled.

After several false starts I decided to write the overrule-*Roe* part of the brief myself, arguing in terms of the jurisprudential illegitimacy of *Roe,* with no discussion of the merits of the right-to-life versus freedom-of-choice dispute. As I expected, the fact that the Solicitor General's office was asking that *Roe* be overruled swamped any disagreements about how we had reached that conclusion.

The brief, filed in mid-July 1985, put me in a leadership position in the Department. I had the support of people inside the Department, of Senator Orrin Hatch, whom I had come to know during an appearance before his committee in the summer of

1984, and particularly of Meese. It seemed to me he liked the Harvard professor from Czechoslovakia with a funny accent. I know he liked the idea that we had attacked *Roe* not on the President's right-to-life grounds but, rather, on neutral, jurisprudential ground. But finally I think it must have been Brad Reynolds' support that was decisive. Backing me must have been painful for him, because mine was the job he himself had wanted more than any other.

A new Solicitor General should be in place in time for the opening of Court in October. While the decision was pending, I had the first of many run-ins with Cooper and Reynolds, whom I later came to call the "federalism police" or the "Holy Office." Our dispute was over a labor case, where I felt that leaving the states free to do as they liked posed a greater threat of overregulation than did giving precedence to federal law. There were several long, fierce meetings with Reynolds, Cooper, and special assistants from the Attorney General's office. I was outnumbered. In the end, I told Reynolds I was unconvinced. I would plan to file my brief, but I would welcome his appealing my decision to our mutual superior, the Attorney General. This happened, and Meese split the baby: the brief would be filed as we had written it, but we would not sign it, only authorize that it be filed in the name of the Labor Board. Our position prevailed in the Supreme Court without a single dissent.[17]

In August the Attorney General called me while I was vacationing, to tell me that the President had decided to nominate me as Solicitor General. In September I paid courtesy calls to the members of the Senate Judiciary Committee. As Acting Solicitor General I had already filed two of the strongest and most controversial briefs of my tenure, the abortion brief and a brief attacking quotas and government-imposed racial preferences.[18] I brought copies of these with me and gave them to each of the Senators I visited. I was surprised by how pleasant and interesting the meetings with the most liberal Democratic Senators—Kennedy, Metzenbaum, Simon—turned out to be. The confirmation hearing in October was serious and useful. Senator Biden asked particularly good questions, and gave me a chance to lay out, more or less impromptu, my conception of the Solicitor General's role and of his relation to the Court, to the President, and to the Attorney General.[19] On October 22, 1985, I was confirmed by unanimous consent.

Solicitor General

As Solicitor General I was responsible for a small but talented staff, and a distinguished institution with 115 years of tradition. Over the last decade some of those traditions had taken an odd turn. The superb career lawyers had gradually come to imagine that the function of the office was so disconnected from the present administration that in fact it was they who should determine what positions were taken, how briefs were written, and who gets hired. Early on I heard complaints from the younger and less subtle members of my staff that I sometimes would talk about a case and form views of it before I had received their staff memo; or that I would produce a first draft of portions of a brief myself and ask a junior to comment on and edit it, rather than the other way around; or that I would consider for career slots persons who had held noncareer—that is, political—positions. They thought the career officials should produce a recommendation or a draft brief, which, if it was done properly, no mere political appointee like myself could in good faith do other than accept. As one of the career deputies had put it, when it was suggested that Attorney General Smith might argue an important case about the exclusionary rule, "The Attorney General represents the administration. We represent the United States."

Up to a point the career lawyers were right. In an important sense government *is* law. This is an ideal that entails a kind of regularity, objectivity, and professional technique apart from—maybe even above—politics. These brilliant and hardworking lawyers had signed up in the service of that ideal. They had not enlisted in the Reagan Revolution. What they consistently failed to see was the extent to which the traditions and precedents of the office had become clogged with commitments and assumptions that were in fact political. I was constantly being told that I should not intervene in cases where all I had to add was a philosophical statement about how the law should come out. I was supposed to represent the interest of "government" in general—that is, the ability of government to go about its work, whatever it may be, as freely as possible. The political bias of this attitude was obscured because since the 1930s the prerogatives of the federal government had been overwhelmingly invoked in furtherance of a liberal, regulatory agenda. But in fact political officers had regularly argued against government prerogative. In *Brown* v. *Board*,[20] the Solicitor General intervened to urge a significant constitutional restriction on the power of government to order society along racial lines. Solicitor General Cox had intervened to urge strict constitutional limits on legislative reapportionment. Solicitor General Thurgood Marshall had urged the strict limits on government power of the *Miranda* rule.[21] It is nothing but politics to celebrate the government's successful intervention in *Brown* but condemn my equally successful intervention in *City of Richmond* v. *Croson*,[22] where the Court struck down the reverse discrimination implicit in some minority business set-asides.

All this is at most half, the dark half, of the story. You cannot put out large amounts of high-quality legal work, scrupulously fair to facts and law, without the kind of lawyers the office had traditionally attracted. My political colleagues in the administration had seen only the dark side. I suppose they thought my status as a Harvard law professor would provide cover for what they hoped would be a wholesale purge. But I was determined to resist a purge that would destroy my ability to be effective. Also, I liked the people I had been working with for half a year, and I saw no need to surround myself with people who shared my commitments. But I did feel the need to make the office my own. My Counselors (for the first nine months Carolyn Kuhl, and for the rest of the time Don Ayer) had joined the office specifically to help me. They shared my general commitments; I could speak to them openly about anything. But the Counselor was just one lawyer out of twenty-two, and that one lawyer's personal loyalty was not enough. Meese wanted more and I did too, though I had a different idea of what that was. What I wanted was to establish my authority as head of the office, but in a way that respected the tradition that career lawyers should be able to work for a conscientious political chief even without sharing his political commitments.

As I walked out of Meese's office after being sworn in, one of his aides stopped me and said how "we" hoped for personnel changes in my office. I am sure the project was to staff this most prestigious of offices with committed, bright conservatives, some of whom would then sit there for as long as the New Deal and Kennedy-Johnson career lawyers had sat there before.[23] Wallace particularly—because of *Bob Jones* and another case, *The Guardians*,[24] which had had to be resolved by Meese several years before in a bitter meeting in the Roosevelt Room of the White House— was seen as a symbol of the enemy within. I said clearly that Wallace had given me no reason to act against him, and until he did I would not touch him. The matter rested there for three weeks, but then the same aide pulled a very solemn face and told me that he and unspecified others were very dissatisfied with the staffing process in the Solicitor General's office— the lack of resignations. I answered only that I was giving a lot of thought to the whole issue.

The immediate question was how to fill a recently vacated Deputy's position. There was a fine, very hardworking career lawyer in the office who badly wanted the promotion. But this lawyer was so much the protégé of the other career Deputies that I felt a real foreboding that if this lawyer were promoted there would be a tight little circle of senior career lawyers and I would be a stranger in my own land. As it was, some of the Deputies had a tendency to give me the drafts of briefs so near to the deadline that I had no real opportunity to make changes or rewrite parts of them. Their work was excellent, and it is as if they felt that there was no need to have yet another hand taken to it. But research and brief-writing were the parts of the job I liked best, and the first name on each brief was mine.

By law, my choice of Deputy must be made as a result of an advertised, open competition. I determined to solve several of my problems at once. I persuaded Louis Cohen—who had been a law clerk to Justice John Harlan and a lecturer at Harvard and Stanford, and was now a senior partner in one of Washington's best law firms—to apply for the job. Though a legal traditionalist, he was certainly not a programmatic conservative. By any standard, however, he was far ahead of all other candidates. Even if he was not what Meese's aides had had in mind, he was exactly what I needed to declare my independence. The appointment had to be approved by Meese. Reynolds supported it, because he saw the advantage of freshness and respected success at the bar. The choice in the end did provoke three resignations, as I predicted it would, but, instead of injuring the office's standards, I had strengthened and deepened them.

It is normal that the Department of Justice should be dominated by the person of the Attorney General. Certainly Ed Meese was a strong and pervasive presence during my years in office. But his friend, adviser, and finally Counselor, Civil Rights chief Brad Reynolds, was just as pervasive a presence, and one I had to deal with sometimes several times a day. Though his official title gave him a quite limited role, in fact he was ubiquitous.

Working with Brad Reynolds was the toughest part of my job—as it had been for Rex Lee. After a confrontation with him you needed a stiff drink and a long walk. I still cannot entirely understand why Brad had this searing, chilling effect on me, especially since I always liked him. In large measure it must have been because of the role that he had chosen to play and the way he found it necessary to play it. A fine business lawyer, he had sought consideration as Anti-Trust chief during the Carter administration, and at the beginning of the Reagan administration he was proposed by his old boss, former Solicitor General Erwin Griswold, to head the Civil, not the Civil Rights Division. Yet sometime early in the administration he had acquired an almost religious sense of mission, and the clarity and fixity with which he saw things compelled him to down doubts and contradictory impulses ruthlessly, first of all in himself and then in others. This was contradicted by the real warmth he felt for all sorts of people who did not agree with him. From the start of the administration his hard edge came from being the man designated to carry forward the part of the Reagan agenda that would arouse the fiercest and most tenacious opposition. I am sure the people who were supposed to work for him in the Civil Rights Division sabotaged his rightful claim to leadership in every way they could, but his situation was not helped by the fact that he did not pick his targets well. He proposed a constant stream of suicidally radical and unconvincing projects, some of which I was then supposed to sell to the Supreme Court. Also, *Bob Jones* had been his special project, and that fact garbled the message he was trying to send. This was the more the pity because he had decent instincts, hated racial prejudice, and had particular warmth for the mentally and physically handicapped, whose rights it was part of his mission to protect.

In later years, after the Senate Judiciary Committee's humiliating rejection of his nomination to be Associate Attorney General, his tenacity took on an increasingly bitter quality. He knew that he had been so vilified that his own government career was in shambles, but he would not abandon his post, or Meese, or ultimately, as he saw it, the President. Perhaps he loved the President as one does a father, and could never forget that Ronald Reagan, the President of the United States, had devoted a five-minute radio broadcast to speak up in his defense. By the end of the Reagan years, balance and restraint of just the sort I had hoped for had been restored to the law of affirmative action. Brad exaggerated and bullied, but maybe that was the only way he could even come near his goals. Perhaps more moderate people like Rex Lee and me would not have arrested the drift toward a quota society. Perhaps only someone who was prepared to be eaten alive could have achieved a half (the proper half) of what he tried to do.

Brad's technique in opposition would be to say little in a meeting, but what he did say dripped scorn and was rich in spoken or implicit accusations of apostasy and unmanly cowardice. And along with the browbeating, he would threaten that, if he did not get his way, then "the AG" would hear about it. At first I found this a little terrifying. The Attorney General had the authority to overrule me, and if that happened too often or dramatically it could be a deadly blow to my authority. I felt strongly that resignation early in my tenure—no matter how lofty the reason—would have been a personal failure. The challenge was to avoid martyrdom while keeping my virtue. My first Counselor, Carolyn Kuhl, was a great help in defusing these confrontations.

By the summer of 1986 I felt that the office was well and truly mine, that I was not a displaced academic masquerading as Solicitor General. And my new Counselor, Don Ayer, to whom Carolyn Kuhl had introduced me, suited my new mood. He and I became adept at sniffing out "neat ideas" that were in truth attempts to lock us into a position or to enforce some unwanted discipline. For example, among the gatherings the AG had organized to consider policy and administrative issues was the Strategic Planning Board, chaired by Brad, which met for a seven o'clock breakfast every other Thursday. In the Board's first months we dealt with interesting general matters and the meetings did not amount to much, except that they were a good way to keep in touch with the heads of some of the other divisions. As time went on, the Board took on a more sinister aspect.

We would talk about some policy issue or about the positions I would take in arguing to the Supreme Court. I could not (and would not have wanted to) object to such discussion. Every morning at eight-thirty there was a general staff meeting presided over by Meese. This meeting followed an eight-fifteen meeting of Meese, Reynolds, and Cribb, from which they emerged as a body to join the larger group. Reynolds would bring to his intimate meeting with Meese what he took to be the consensus of the breakfast group, and then announce it at the larger meeting. This implied that the supposed consensus position reached over breakfast had been discussed and approved in private by the Attorney General and was now being announced as a directive. This was, in effect, an attempt to shift authority away from me, which I found intolerable. I was ready to listen to anybody, but the final decision must be mine until specifically overruled by the Attorney General. As Don Ayer and I saw this end run developing, I determined to head it off at once, and went to Meese to tell him that I did not question his authority to overrule me but would not accept an oblique challenge to my authority either. He listened and assured me that I had misunderstood what was intended to be only a way of increasing collegiality among the Department's leadership. After that the breakfasts were a good bit more relaxed—and less well attended, though I rarely missed one.

Attorney General Meese

Ed Meese was the most elusive and important personality on the Department's scene. His support helped me to do my job—to write the briefs and to hire the people I wanted. During my tenure there were suggestions that I write or support briefs on pornography, on resurrecting the death penalty in a notorious espionage case, on applying a murder statute retroactively to Yassir Arafat, that I file a brief urging the overruling of *Runyon* v. *McCrary*,[25] an established though initially dubious civil-rights precedent, or briefs supporting a state law requiring the teaching of "creation science,"[26] and supporting the criminalization of flag burning.[27] None of these suggestions came from Meese; nor could I even detect his fingerprints. And if a dispute reached him and I was firm, he backed me up every time.

The *Miranda* episode is a good example of our dealings. Meese had made some notorious remarks about the *Miranda* rule,[28] the most unfortunate of which was that the rule helped only those who had something to hide. His judgment on *Miranda*'s jurisprudential and theoretical unsoundness was—or originally had been—widely shared. After all, John Harlan, the most professionally respected Justice in the postwar years, had dissented bitterly in *Miranda,* and the American Law Institute—an establishment law-reform group of lawyers, academics, and judges—had only a short time before the *Miranda* decision considered a much more moderate and flexible solution to the problem of police questioning.[29] The nakedly legislative nature of the *Miranda* rules was obviously inappropriate to a decision purporting to interpret and apply general constitutional requirements; in this *Miranda* resembled *Roe* v. *Wade.* On the other hand, most professional law-enforcement organizations had learned to live with *Miranda,* and even to love it, to the extent that it provided them with a safe harbor: if they followed the rules, they had a fair assurance that a confession would be admissible and a conviction built on it would stick. The menace of *Miranda* came from overzealous judges, suspicious of all confessions and maybe even of the machinery of the criminal law in general. Those judges, instead of treating *Miranda* as a legislative compromise, would reason from it by analogy to exclude confessions in cases where the police had complied literally with its rules. A dramatic example,

Colorado v. *Connelly,*[30] had seen a state court's use of *Miranda* to overturn a conviction where the defendant had walked up to a policeman on the street and confessed to a murder because "God had told him to." Rex Lee and I (though not the Carter Justice Department) had regularly entered state and federal cases like *Connelly* to urge that *Miranda* be confined to the literal rule it had enacted: before the police question a suspect in custody, they must warn him that he had a right to remain silent and to consult a lawyer. We resisted extensions to cases like *Connelly* or to cases where the police did not tell the suspect what crime they were investigating,[31] or even that a lawyer hired by the suspect's family was trying to see him.[32] And we generally succeeded—with Justices Brennan and Marshall in dissent.

Meese's minions had taken up the cry and now proclaimed it a Department objective to get the Supreme Court to overrule *Miranda.* Most experienced federal prosecutors in and out of my office were opposed to this project, as was I. We were afraid that a frontal assault of this sort would offend Justices Powell and O'Connor, thereby jeopardizing the progress we had made in taming and confining the *Miranda* rule. The rigorists finally brought matters to a head: the Attorney General called a meeting of some twenty persons from throughout the Department. One after another, the rigorists pronounced their anathemas on the *Miranda* rule, while the professional prosecutors sat silently by, thinking, I suppose, that this was not their show. But it was my show. I knew that this meeting could end up in a directive to launch a frontal attack on *Miranda* on the next possible occasion. So I spoke up: I didn't mind dropping atom bombs, but not on my own troops. This was not *Roe,* where we have had strong dissents while the substantive constitutional doctrine was getting worse and worse. Here not a single Justice had indicated any interest in overruling *Miranda,* while the substantive law was getting better and better.

Meese ruled from the bench: apart from some soothing and largely irrelevant qualifications, we would carry on as before. Afterward, I went to Meese privately and told him that I felt sure that the story of the meeting would leak to the press (as it did),[33] and that I did not want to look good at his expense; would he allow me to give an attributed interview to *The New York Times* laying out the substance of his decision? He agreed—and for the rest of my time in office the *Miranda* issue was laid to rest.

In these and other meetings I found Meese intelligent, receptive, and intellectually curious. He enjoyed the give and take of technical legal discussion. And in a disagreement, if you stood your ground he would not push an unreasonable or extreme position. During the first year and a half of his tenure he organized conferences for Department leaders on federalism, economic liberty, and separation of powers, in which outside academics would participate as well. He would sit through all the discussions diligently taking notes, and at the end would give a fair and full summary.

Yet something went wrong. Meese was one of the most vilified personalities in the Reagan administration—a man who attracted all the hatred and contempt which the establishment felt for the President but were inhibited from expressing. The caricature that emerged in the media bore little relation to reality, but there were aspects of the public portrait that were drawn from life. His dealings with the ubiquitous Bob Wallach, who quite publicly held himself out as a conduit to his friend Ed Meese,[34] and Meese's chaotic personal financial dealings, as catalogued in the first Independent Counsel's report, showed some blind spot in his field of ethical vision.[35] Still, I sat with the Attorney General every day in a staff meeting of some dozen people, lunched with him, the Director of the FBI, and a few other officials almost every week, attended numerous meetings for special purposes, and had dozens of private conversations with him, and I never got the impression he was a grasping or venal person. If anything, he seemed rather careless of his personal situation—not vain, not greedy, not even particularly eager for acclaim.

But carelessness does not account for Meese's troubles either; there must have been a more serious flaw. In discussions of intricate legal problems, he grasped and held in mind a large number of details. The failing was probably less carelessness than an odd lack of rigor that allowed him to overlook faults in a person, a project, or a situation. I had the sense that he was adept at telling himself stories to excuse or explain away what was inconvenient. And, as is often the case, this sentimental lack of rigor went along with great personal warmth and genuine kindness.

I did not encounter his failings in my own dealings with Meese. This is not to say I deny their existence— indeed, it was my most disagreeable duty as Acting Attorney General in July 1988 (after the Attorney General had announced his intention to resign) to receive the second Independent Counsel's report on Meese and to refer it to the Department's Office of

Professional Responsibility. What is most striking for me now, as I try to make sense of my experiences, is just this disparity between my own observations and aspects of the public record. I am tempted to conclude that either my observations or the public record must be seriously mistaken—they cannot both be right. Yet the most important lesson may just be how people, particularly people in public life, combine quite contradictory and apparently incompatible qualities.

But personal failings also do not entirely explain the way things unraveled. Meese was a lightning rod. The Reagan administration tried to make a revolution. It proposed dismantling large parts of the welfare-bureaucratic state which had grown up over the previous half-century. Revolutionary as it was, it required (in Danton's phrase) boldness, more boldness, ever more boldness. And Ed Meese did not strike me as a basically audacious person. (His friend and mentor, Ronald Reagan, was an improbable revolutionary too.) Meese was too good a lawyer to be easy as a revolutionary. Yet, given the legal and constitutional nature of the revolution, his presence at the head of the troops was indispensable. It is hard for me today—as it was when we would debate particular positions and actions—to be sure just how personally committed Meese was to all aspects of this revolutionary program. Certainly, when I balked at making what seemed to me extreme or unsupportable or unwise or incorrect arguments, the Attorney General backed me up.[36] He showed caution and hesitation. But in spite of this, he was associated with extreme positions—so much so that the bench and bar were alarmed into opposing Meese more strongly than his own dispositions warranted, and certainly more than was tactically desirable from the point of view of attaining the goals of the revolution.

Meese gave a number of provocative speeches early in his term: to the annual meeting of the American Bar Association in July 1985,[37] suggesting that the Supreme Court had taken a wrong turn fifty years ago on federalism and on the application of the Bill of Rights to the states; to the Federal Bar Association in September 1985,[38] questioning the constitutionality of the well-established independent regulatory agencies;[39] in a speech at Tulane Law School, recalling that there is a distinction between the Constitution and constitutional law as developed by the Supreme Court;[40] to the Federalist Society on interpreting the Constitution according to the intent of its framers.[41] Taken singly and stated by a scholar wielding no authority, these positions would all have been quite acceptable. As speeches delivered by the Attorney General of the United States, they put the cat among the pigeons in the worst way, as I found when questioned by Justice Sandra Day O'Connor in the course of an otherwise successful argument in the Gramm-Rudman case.[42] Meese's predecessor in the Reagan administration, Attorney General William French Smith, almost certainly held the same views, but he was a reassuringly drab speaker, with a corporate lawyer's instinct for avoiding the sensational. Coming from Attorney General Meese, these speeches were a provocation from which he and his program scarcely recovered. Why did he do it?

I suspect that Meese's miscalculation came in part from an impulse to berate an elite orthodoxy that was vulnerable on intellectual grounds and had dealt harshly with him and his friend Ronald Reagan. In this he was more egged on than counseled by his personal advisers. I suspect they felt strongly that they were right, and that the liberal orthodoxies in the bar and the media had up until now monopolized the debate, so that, if for a change they had a bully pulpit, public opinion would swing their way. And in this they made the disastrous mistake of underestimating the strength of both their opponents' arguments and their opponents' ability to fight back.

Also, however, it is not quite true that Meese did it. These speeches were written for Meese by his cadre of committed young assistants. Because those who were standing with or behind the Attorney General thought of themselves as revolutionaries, they did not trust the usual channels to deliver results. The bureaucracy could not be trusted to implement a revolutionary program. I and other political appointees could not be trusted completely: unlike the very young members of the inner circle, we were not creatures of the movement; we had careers and established positions to which we could return and against which we measured our performance. And heads of offices, as I was, are notoriously vulnerable to the staffs they depend on to accomplish their day-to-day activities. Even the Attorney General could not be fully trusted. The relentless pressure of public attention and vilification wears down the most committed leader. And perhaps Meese showed a certain softness at the core of his revolutionary will.

The provocative public statements served a purpose; they pushed the Attorney General so far out on a limb that he was committed. Though they attracted criticism from the general media, these speeches would make him a hero in the eyes of the hard-core faithful, isolating him from the center while binding him tighter to the fringe. And the speeches were a way to impose a degree of conformity on subordinates in independently responsible offices, without putting the Attorney General to the trouble of explicitly overruling their decisions. The numerous collegial gatherings, like Brad's breakfasts, were another way to convey this pressure for conformity outside of regular channels. I remember our weekend conference on federalism at Williamsburg. The discussion was serious and interesting. The presence of outside scholars made it hard to think of this as a cabal. Yet a subtle menace hung in the air. So, when Richard Willard raised a caveat against leaving too much authority to the states, because the same social forces that had produced overregulation in federal programs were hard at work at the state level and could sometimes only be resisted by uniform federal standards, this seemed like defiance of the Holy Office.

In the end, it was not revolutionary zeal that brought Meese down. A more ruthless and effective politician would have jettisoned Reynolds after the Senate repudiated him in the summer of 1985. Instead Meese added immeasurably to his own difficulties by promoting Reynolds to the position of Counselor to the Attorney General, while keeping him on as head of the Civil Rights Division. (The same might be said of his tolerance of my resistance to some of his proclaimed objectives.) Alternating between provocation and sentimentality is always dangerous to a politician, but fatal to a man who had gone out of his way to make himself the symbol of everything that enraged the liberal establishment. On March 29, 1988, the Deputy Attorney General, Arnold Burns, and my old friend and former student

Bill Weld, the chief of the Criminal Division, resigned. They let it be known that they believed that the Attorney General's involvement with Bob Wallach had so far compromised his moral authority that he should leave. Burns had earlier called (as was his duty according to the Ethics in Government Act[43]) for an Independent Counsel to consider whether there was any basis for prosecuting Meese in connection with the Wallach matter. Wallach himself had recently been indicted. And the calls in the press and Congress for Meese's removal were growing louder. As intended, the resignations created a storm that eventually blew Meese out of office.

Since I was now the most senior officer left after Meese,[44] there was great pressure for me to resign too. It came from Meese's enemies, who felt that the Solicitor General's resignation—an unprecedented event—would surely bring Meese down. And it came from the media (TV crews waited outside my front door in the morning), who hoped for a continuing crescendo in the Washington soap opera they love to concoct out of serious public events. Whatever my opinion about whether the Attorney General should resign because of the wounds he had suffered— honorable, treacherous, and self-inflicted—I felt strongly that *I* should not. The Deputy Attorney General is meant to be the Attorney General's daily collaborator and alter ego. Bill Weld was in charge of the Department's criminal work and had come to the conclusion that as a prosecutor he would have sought Meese's indictment—something the Independent Counsel declined to do.[45] By contrast, I had no personal involvement with these issues. They had nothing to do with my work. Indeed, by any standard, my office was humming along better than ever, and Meese had consistently backed the decisions I had made to maintain its integrity and quality. So, if I had resigned, it would have been a political gesture, not a judgment about my ability to do my work and run my office. I took the advice of a number of experienced and disinterested elders outside the office, who all confirmed my sense that my resignation would just involve the Solicitor General's office in a political imbroglio of a sort the office had always avoided.

I did owe it to Meese to tell him frankly what I thought he should do, and also what I would do myself. I may not report the substance of our two private conversations, but I will say that he received me with a friendly and studied consideration I very much doubt I or many people could have managed in the circumstances.*

In March 1988 I lunched with Boyden Gray, then counsel to Vice-President Bush, to tell him that the new President, whoever he might be, should have his own Solicitor General. For me, four years of molding a presence as Ronald Reagan's Solicitor General were enough. I told Gray that on January 20, 1989, I would resign, to start teaching again on February 1.

---

* This episode led to what I regret most deeply about my own conduct in office. During those pressured days I sought the advice of, among others, retired Justice Lewis Powell, and I discussed the situation with a number of friends in and out of the Solicitor General's office. Because I was not careful enough about what I said to whom, *The New York Times* learned about my conversation with Justice Powell and also something of my advice to Attorney General Meese. Some of my admirers supposed I had leaked both stories. I had not.

2

INTERPRETATION

In a faithful interpretation, the performer's own personality and his need for expression come into play essentially as a medium through which the work can be made public. . . . Authenticity dispenses with all this guesswork and uncertainty. . . . We no longer try to infer what Bach would have liked; instead we ascertain how he was played in his lifetime. . . . This substitutes . . . research for sympathy, and it makes a study of the conditions of the old performance more urgent than a study of the text.[1]

*T*he framers of the Constitution would certainly be surprised by the state of constitutional law today. It was only fifty years ago, for instance, that the First Amendment liberties of speech and religion began to be applied to the states. The gradual development of constitutional law became an explosion of change in the Warren Court. With a liberal majority firmly in control in the middle sixties, the Warren Court caused a thick growth of rights and rights doctrine to grow up around what may originally have seemed like isolated decisions striking at extreme and uncivilized acts of government. For instance, what started as the Court's gagging at death sentences imposed on men from whom confessions had been tortured, had become, by the time of *Mapp* and *Miranda,* an intricate constitutional code of police conduct. Similarly, from the early germs of decision in *Pierce* v. *Society of Sisters*[2] (1925) and *Meyer* v. *Nebraska*[3] (1923)—cases that recognized the right of parents to educate their children in private schools and in the language of their choice—grew up a body of doctrine constitutionalizing many parts of family law previously thought to be the secure preserve of state authority. In the reapportionment cases[4] the Court undertook to supervise the makeup and electoral scheme of every legislature, board, and commission in the country, imposing a rigid rule of equal representation that Articles I and II of the Constitution, setting up the Senate and the Electoral College, would clearly have failed.

This rapid growth in constitutional rights was unsettling. So when *Roe* came along—with all the fervor attached to the abortion issue—many were inclined to lump everything together into a generalized complaint against "what the Supreme Court is doing to us." This was a mistake. Some of what the Supreme Court had been doing was right: for instance, projecting into present circumstances the constitutional principles of the First Amendment,[5] or demanding full equality before the law regardless of race. After all, several of the landmark cases were joined or even written by conservative Justices such as John Harlan. And what was wrong with cases like *Roe* was not peculiar to the Supreme Court—it was just that the Supreme Court's status elevated its decisions above reversal in any other court and gave them special notoriety.

The Law Gone Wrong

The law had gone wrong. Courts should be the impartial tool for doing justice between man and man. They should guarantee our liberties by telling us firmly and clearly where we stand, and so hold all of us—including the government—to the bargain of social life. Instead, the federal courts had become political engines of the left-liberal agenda. *Roe* was just a dramatic example of a system of judging that had run badly off the rails. I believe it was distress at this general phenomenon that fueled not only the effort to overturn *Roe,* but also a more general insistence on doctrines and principles to discipline the wanderings of a federal judiciary almost half of whose members had been appointed during the brief incumbency of Jimmy Carter[6]—with at least as much an eye to politics and philosophy as the appointments of the Reagan years.

That something had gone wrong could best be seen

in hundreds of lower federal-court decisions. The Supreme Court decides some 150 cases a year and because of its status and prominence cannot escape controversy. In reality if not in theory, however, those lower federal courts have the last word; the tens of thousands of cases they decide each year weave the fabric of the law we live by.

Some of these were the decisions of individual federal trial judges—like Judge Brevard Hand's decision purporting to overrule decades of Supreme Court precedent in order to allow spoken prayer in public schools, or the Texas federal judge who found there was a constitutional right to take part in high-school spring training.[7] But others came from panels of federal appellate judges, an elite corps numbering 168, whose decisions are deliberate and calculated acts requiring written opinions. For instance, the Ninth Circuit Court of Appeals was determined to right a wrong it felt had been done to a group of Philippine "scouts" who had been promised U.S. citizenship for their resistance to the Japanese occupation during World War II. Three times the Supreme Court had to reverse that court's decision to grant the scouts citizenship, because the decision was contrary to law. And twice the lower-court judges were prepared to publish opinions that were a transparent evasion of their duty to follow the Supreme Court's decree.[8]

At other times courts have been willing to twist not only legal doctrine but common sense in order to get to a result they felt was substantively just. Such a case was *United States* v. *Hohri,* where the full bench of the District of Columbia Court of Appeals was willing to say—over vigorous dissents—that a lawsuit started almost forty years after the fact somehow complied with a rule that lawsuits must be started within six years. This offense to common sense was committed for the sympathetic purpose of helping get compensation to the Japanese-Americans unjustly interned during World War II.[9] These are not isolated examples; they can be multiplied.[10]

What is so bad about these cases? It may be that all government power is borrowed power, but the power a judge holds over us is lent on very precise terms: the laws themselves are the terms of that loan. If the judge exercises power contrary to those terms, he is an embezzler, even if he takes from the rich to give to the poor—unless you believe our society is so corrupt that the terms of the trust are not worthy of respect, and none of the judges in the cases I refer to make such an assumption. Since all other government power over us is ultimately subject to being checked by the courts, if we cannot know where we stand with them then our liberty is only as sure as the whims and politics of judges.

The Rule of Law

The ideal behind my intuitive picture of how judges should decide is the liberal ideal of the rule of law, which holds that men of intelligence and reasonable good will can come to a fair measure of agreement about what the law is, and that our liberty is most secure when in the end it is to the rule of law that government power is responsible. This is the ideal against which I measure the work of the Supreme Court and offer a theory of judging and of constitutional interpretation.

The rule of law is not quite a law of rules,[11] but it is a law of rules, principles, customs, practices, and understandings. It is law responsible to criteria that in the end we can learn and communicate to others. It may be as definite as a rule, or as tacit as the understanding of language by a native speaker. Still, it always has an important measure of definiteness; the law is something one can come to know, and knowledgeable people can tell good from bad law. Most important, law is not the same as policy. It is policy disciplined by a public, external standard. This is not to say that the rule of law means the law cannot change, only that when we change the law we must do so publicly and then bind ourselves to the new rules. Law may change, but not retroactively, and not so fast that it cannot serve as a guide at all. How public, how prospective, how stable, how learnable the law need be are questions about what criteria satisfy the ideal of rule of law. But there are no criteria about criteria. At some point criteria of stability and clarity run out, and you just know. There is good faith and bad faith. The decisions in cases like *Hohri* or the Philippine scouts, for instance, were made in bad faith.

The rule of law is the reciprocal of liberty. Though the laws restrict liberty, without rules liberty cannot exist. The rule of law came into focus along with our modern idea of liberty. The main point is simple. If we know where we stand, we can adapt our conduct accordingly. Law, to be law, must let us know where we stand. And this is an ideal profoundly at war with the ideal of equality of result: if people are free except as the rules constrain them, then some will inevitably find their way to a better life than others. If you knock them flat again, you will be breaking the bargain which they kept by playing by the rules. Many of us who tried to bring the law around were ultimately defending the concept of liberty, just as Justice Brennan, one of the most effective proponents of the progressive agenda, was advocating equality of outcome.[12] For the rule of law opposes every attempt to define justice in terms of end results: how the world must end up looking, how people must be, and how they must stand in relation to one another. When the Massachusetts Constitution of 1780[13] gave as the end of its ordinance "that we be a government of laws and not men," it surely meant that it was "men" who imposed substantive patterns and ends on one another, whereas laws were the laws of freedom.

Originalism

In this context originalism—the doctrine that the Constitution should be interpreted according to the intent of its framers[14]—was not a quirk. Although it almost became the motto of the Meese Justice Department, when Judge Bork first voiced the concept in his 1971 Harris Lectures at Indiana Law School[15] he was responding above all to the dissolution of the ideal of law among legal intellectuals. But he was also responding to his own disappointment at his inability to find in reason itself any criterion to serve as the anchor for the rule of law.[16] Originalism sought its anchor in the definiteness not just of a text but of a historical truth about that text: what particular persons intended by the words they used. Why Bork, and those who followed him,[17] wanted definiteness, an anchor, we know. Why the seemingly factual definiteness of historic truth was thought to supply such an anchor is also obvious. That the concept of original intent cannot provide that anchor is only slightly less obvious. What is not obvious at all is where else we can anchor the law, and particularly constitutional law.

The concept of originalism speaks to the most basic legal question: by what authority do judges impose their views on the people, even to the point of striking down laws made by the people's elected representatives? The first step in the argument (John Marshall's argument in *Marbury* v. *Madison*[18]), though perhaps not inevitable,[19] is strongly grounded in the text that established us as a nation: "This Constitution, and the Laws of the United States which shall be made in Pursuance thereof . . . shall be the supreme Law of the Land; and the Judges in every state shall be bound thereby." So, in doing their jobs, judges cannot avoid interpreting the Constitution. It is only the next step that is controversial: if interpretation is to maintain the line between the power judges exercise and the source of that power, it must be a straight line. For the originalists the only line that is straight enough is the one that compels interpretation in accordance with the intent of the framers. The originalist impulse is to turn interpretation into a factual inquiry about what particular people thought about the meaning of a particular text. Though there are admitted difficulties in getting at the facts, at least it is an inquiry that is supposed to have the virtue of being about historical facts.

The objections to this reasoning are devastating. First, there is no way to identify who should count as framers without making just the kind of judgments this technique is supposed to spare us. This is illustrated by the originalist practice of using *The Federalist Papers* as strong evidence of the framers' intent. Those eighty-five essays on politics and the Constitution are certainly among the jewels of American political reflection—the music of reason. But it is their intrinsic worth, not their authenticity as evidence of the state of mind of everyone who in the end voted on the ratification of the Constitution, that makes them so persuasive. The *Federalist* authors—Hamilton, Jay, Madison—were a faction, writing to persuade principally the citizens of New York to ratify the proposed Constitution.[20] More to the point are the records of the Convention itself, held secret and unpublished for more than two decades. But that only sharpens the question: why should the undisclosed debates and reflections of the draftsmen of the document take on legislative force when the document itself has force not as an act of *their* wills but, rather, by the act of the state conventions that ratified the Constitution? As with *The Federalist Papers,* the most that can be said of these records is that they illuminate the constitutional text by showing us the thought of the wisest men who had occasion to think most deeply about it. But that is an interpretive, not a factual judgment—albeit a very sensible one.

Furthermore, there is good reason to believe that the interpretive traditions at the time of the framing strongly rejected recourse to extrinsic materials to fix the meaning of public texts.[21] That is one reason why Madison kept his notes of the Convention unpublished for so long, and why the delegates to the Convention bound themselves not to reveal the contents of their proceedings.[22] Behind this interpretive tradition stands a philosophy of language. Language must have a public meaning if it is to order our common life. The subjective intentions of the few million voters who passed on the constitutional text are therefore not only unascertainable but beside the point. It is a public text they put in force, and it is as a public text we must try to understand it.

This argument might be taken to say that we should consult historical usage, as we would a dictionary, to get at the late-eighteenth-century Anglo-American meaning of constitutional language.[23] Though the Court has in fact done that in a few areas—for instance, to determine when the Seventh Amendment requires a jury trial in civil cases[24]—it has not felt bound by original practice and assumptions when dealing with the more general terms: whether indecent speech, theater, or nonverbal expression is covered by the guarantee of free speech,[25] or whether wage regulation in manufacturing industries was regulation of "commerce among the several states,"[26] or whether flogging or capital punishment would be prohibited by the Eighth Amendment as "cruel and unusual."[27] Even as to these more open-ended terms, the originalist would stick to historical practice and understanding whenever they are clear and specific enough to answer the question posed by the case at hand. Only if there is not or could not be such a historical understanding (there can have been no nineteenth-century understanding about wiretapping or low-flying airplanes[28]) may we extrapolate from historical materials, and then only to the extent necessary to make the history applicable to the case at hand. Judge Bork suggested this in one of the best and most considered statements of his originalism,[29] and Justice Scalia proposed this approach in an analogous context in *Michael H. and Victoria D.* v. *Gerald D.*[30] Judge Bork's method would mean reversing *Griswold* v. *Connecticut* (the case thought to establish the constitutional right to privacy, holding unconstitutional a Connecticut law criminalizing the use of contraceptives) and probably *Brown* v. *Board,* since at the time of the framing of the Fourteenth Amendment there was a very general understanding that it was within the power of the state to impose morals legislation of the sort struck down in *Griswold,* and separate but "equal" public schooling. Justices O'Connor and Kennedy kept the Court from subscribing to this test in the *Gerald D.* case, finding it "inconsistent with our past decisions." They would not "foreclose the unanticipated by the imposition of a single mode of historical analysis."

But it is not just that this method is out of line with how the Court has always worked; it is a method that really does not deliver what it promises. It does not give us the empirical, nonjudgmental rigor to which originalism aspires. The proposal concedes the main premise of any nonoriginalist method by permitting us to infer general principles from specific constitutional provisions and then apply those principles to new cases. Second, the line it would draw between cases where the originalist method is and is not applicable is an illusory one. It is not just technology that changes, giving us the problem of wiretapping. Legal contexts change too, so that measures which in isolation appear identical tell quite different stories in their new surroundings. Sorting all this out requires just the sort of judgments originalism is meant to spare us.

Lawyers' Law[31]

Originalism was not the original interpretive doctrine of the framers nor of the framing generation. It was taken for granted that the Constitution, like other legal texts, would be interpreted by men who were learned in the law, arguing cases and writing judgments in the way lawyers and judges had done for centuries in England and its colonies.[32] Argument from precedent and by analogy would allow the Constitution to be applied to changing circumstances. There was certainly no notion that every new circumstance would be resolved by invoking the amendment process.

As Solicitor General, Judge Bork had much the same experience I did—reading, editing, and sometimes writing hundreds of briefs as the head of a busy appellate law office. That experience taught me that, even in constitutional cases, precedent and analogy are the stuff of legal argument, and that legal argument is what moves the Court—or moves it when all involved are doing their work right. Certainly the Justices sometimes ignore or run over or through the arguments, but when this happens it is felt as unfair and wrong. And judges too must feel that precedent and analogy are the straw out of which their bricks are made. A brief to the Court is largely analogy and precedent. (I used to tease the lawyers in my office that the ideal SG's brief would have not one word that is not in quotation marks and attributed to some prior Supreme Court opinion.) This has been the texture of common lawyers' reasoning for centuries.

However, this will not seem much of a method if what you are looking for is a set of rules so palpable and constraining that they will be proof against chicanery, evasion, and disingenuousness. But no set of rules is proof against that. Human beings made a bargain with uncertainty a long time ago; no enterprise of any complexity, richness, or subtlety can be ordered by rules as unbending as iron and as heavy as lead. The use of rules to coordinate human enterprises of every sort assumes a generous and honest attitude. The more the system of rules sets out to make itself proof against evasion, and the more it makes the ideal rule that which even a fool or a scoundrel must either follow or openly defy, the more the society must resemble a prison camp. The method I identify assumes intelligence and good faith—that is a strength, not a weakness, and more shame to him who abuses it. So I understand the connection that is perceived between originalism and the rule of law, but it is a connection that rests on a mistake—on a mistake and on too grim a view of human nature and of human intelligence.

Finally, I am also puzzled by the originalist celebration of majority rule as the presumed default source of law, from which one may only depart on the clearest textual warrant in the Constitution, a warrant underwritten by the intent of the framers. The originalists belong to the party of liberty—as do I—so it is odd to see them repair to majority rule, which has not often been seen as a very secure haven of liberty, and certainly was not seen as such by the framers. The framing generation would soon have the French Revolution to show that majority rule, pure and direct, was a will-o'-the-wisp, the pursuit of which could only end in calamity for justice, for tranquillity, for prosperity, for liberty—the things they really cared about. The sense in which the Constitution is based on the consent of the governed is complex and structured. The authority, powers, and methods of John Marshall's judiciary were—and are—entirely appropriate to it.

Continuity and Change

In 1937, the year after Roosevelt's second-term landslide, the Supreme Court handed down two remarkable decisions: *West Coast Hotel* v. *Parrish*[33] and *NLRB* v. *Jones & Laughlin Corp.*[34] These decisions marked a major turn in constitutional jurisprudence. For forty years the Court had put major but uncertain constitutional impediments in the way of government regulation of the economy, and, more particularly, impediments to the federal government's role in such regulation. These two decisions have generally seemed so abrupt and drastic as to put in doubt the stability and neutrality of constitutional jurisprudence, but I believe that such cynical doubts are unwarranted.[35]

The Supreme Court's turn was not motivated just by a change of policy or an act of will. Along with a change of heart came a change of mind. The categories that needed to be elaborated in order to distinguish proper from improper economic regulation in a sensible way had themselves become more and more complicated, unperspicuous, arbitrary. As we learned more about the economy, and as the economy became increasingly interrelated and national, the old concepts the Court had invoked to confine national regulation just could not bear the weight that was put on them. The same is true of limitations on the power of governments (national or state) to regulate economic relations at all. The same developments that made the economy indisputably national also displayed the economy as inextricably conventional,[36] made up of a web of relations which government in part creates, in part sustains, always meddles in. For these reasons, the Court's previous program could not be sustained intellectually—at least not without requiring an unraveling of arrangements and understandings more radical than anyone could contemplate. The New Deal *did* pose a challenge, but it was as much an intellectual as a political challenge to the Court's jurisprudence.

And there was far more continuity in the Court's jurisprudence than a cynical political interpretation acknowledges. On national power, the Court's supposed new turn might well be thought to hark back to early decisions by Chief Justice Marshall.[37] Similarly, the naturalness of government interference in economic expectations may well have been settled a hundred years earlier in the *Charles River Bridge* case.[38] Thus the Court's 1937 turn was not at all unrooted in the past. Just as significantly, the 1937 decisions were not so much a retreat of the Court from the scene as a shift in emphasis to aspects of liberty that seemed more amenable to coherent doctrinal elaboration and better rooted in the sources of the Court's own legitimacy. Where these sources and methods have implications for economic relations, the Court has shown that it will not hesitate to intervene again—as the development of First Amendment protections for commercial speech shows.[39]

Brown v. *Board of Education* is an example of doctrine and constitutional right growing rather than shrinking. Here again I would answer the cynics that this growth owes at least as much to the internal pressure of established constitutional principles as to political imperatives. When *Brown* first came out, there was a good deal of academic dispute about the original understanding regarding segregated schools at the time of the Fourteenth Amendment.[40] Those who argue that the post–Civil War national community accepted segregation as sensible and constitutional are more likely to have history on their side. But the Court's decision in *Brown* is sufficiently justified if we may conclude that segregation was inconsistent with the Fourteenth Amendment's equal-protection language, understood as stating a broad and organizing (reorganizing) principle. As in the case of national power over the economy, subsequent events drove the fallacy of the prior separate-but-equal doctrine out into the open.

Those who think there is nothing between the naked willfulness of judicial policy-making and inescapable, empirical iron rules will be disappointed by this account. But as the story of originalism shows, they are bound to be disappointed anyway. Whatever stories we may have told ourselves, the Reagan administration's project of judicial restraint in the end could be no more than a project to reintroduce a conception of law disciplined by a respect for tradition, professionalism, and careful, candid reasoning.

3

PRIVACY

Due process has not been reduced to any formula; its content cannot be determined by reference to any code. The best that can be said is that through the course of this Court's decisions it has represented the balance which our Nation, built upon the postulates of respect for the liberty of individuals, has struck between that liberty and the demands of organized society. If the supplying of content to the Constitutional concept has of necessity been a rational process, it certainly has not been one where the judges have felt free to roam where unguided speculation might take them.[1]

*T*he Reagan administration made *Roe* v. *Wade* the symbol of everything that had gone wrong in law, particularly in constitutional law. And the constitutional right of privacy was seen as the deep theoretical root of the trouble. We undertook to get *Roe* overruled. *Roe* was wrong in method and result. But the attack on the constitutional right of privacy was misconceived. It grew out of the same disappointed yearning for a mechanical rule of judging that gave us originalism. That is a part of the project I never signed on to.

The seminal statement of the constitutional right to privacy is Justice Harlan's dissent in *Poe* v. *Ullman*. In that opinion he concluded that a Connecticut statute prohibiting the use of contraceptives even by married couples deprived those couples of liberty in violation of the Fourteenth Amendment. Although the opinion is celebrated today as a landmark in the expansive reading of the Constitution, it was motivated as much by a contrary impulse: Justice Harlan was joined in a continuing dispute with Justice Hugo Black, who held that the Fourteenth Amendment incorporated the Bill of Rights more or less in its entirety and applied it to the states.[2]

Justice Black was deeply suspicious—as are the originalists—of constitutional arguments that go beyond the literal text. He saw such fancy arguments mainly as a way of denying people the full measure of protection from state and local governments that the Bill of Rights originally gave them from the national government. After all, these nonliteral techniques had been used to frustrate the early stage of the New Deal. But nonmechanical, more traditional techniques had also been invoked by judges who were not averse to economic regulation and were concerned about civil liberties. Justice Cardozo in *Palko* v. *Connecticut*[3] and Justice Frankfurter in *Rochin* v. *California*[4] had acknowledged that due process places restraints on what the state may do to people, but they thought the due-process clause assured only the limitations implicit in the concept of "ordered liberty," limitations such as would be generally recognized by "civilized peoples" according to "evolving" concepts of "decency." The Bill of Rights itself was addressed only to Congress, and to Cardozo, Frankfurter, and Harlan this meant that the relatively precise, sometimes technical prohibitions of the Bill of Rights do not extend literally to the states. For instance, many civilized nations do not recognize the privilege against self-incrimination—at least not with all the highly restrictive details worked out by the Supreme Court. Justice Black scolded Frankfurter and Harlan with that day's version of the charge of judicial activism: their methods substituted uncertain ethical speculation for literal reading of an authoritative text. The dispute, then, was between a kind of anti-intellectual, textual fundamentalism and Justice Harlan's belief in the possibility—indeed, inevitability—of reasoning and judgment in applying the Constitution.

Poe attracted Harlan in part because it showed that at times his own method was more protective of personal liberty than Black's. To his mind, the Fourteenth Amendment was clearly a warrant for protecting "life, liberty and property" against extreme and unfair impositions. A truly literal reading of the Amendment could offer no protection at all against general legislation, since legislative impositions would by definition be authorized by law (the statute), and whatever was done according to statute would be by "due process of law." Much in the history as well as the earliest interpretations of the Amendment assumed that its protections went beyond assuring mere procedural regularity and at times would be substantive—hence the apparent oxymoron "substantive due process." To Harlan's way of thinking, incorporating the Bill of Rights into due process was a trick giving the impression of literalism, a trick that just was not candid about the necessity for judgment and reasoning in interpreting the Due Process Clause.

Harlan saw no escape from the method of reason. Patrician and conservative, he had confidence in himself and in the work of judges acting conscientiously and by traditional methods. The words of the Constitution were the starting point, but different provisions invited different breadths of interpretation, and even relatively precise terms might require considerable judgment in their application. In interpreting the broad language of the Fourteenth Amendment, the Constitution as a whole should serve as a guide. The particular guarantees specified in the Bill of Rights are like the points on a graph, which the judge joins by a line to describe a coherent and rationally compelling function. Harlan found such points in the Fourth Amendment's protection of the privacy of the home and in the Fifth Amendment's protection against state intrusion to compel self-incrimination, and in the Speech, Assembly, and Religion Clauses. From these he had already extrapolated a constitutional liberty of association in *NAACP* v. *Alabama*,[5] and the Court long ago had referred to them to limit intrusions upon family life.

However, he made clear that the object was not to

proclaim the most sweeping and exciting principle, but to find a rational basis for deciding the case at hand. In the end Harlan emphasized that the Connecticut statute was unconstitutional because it authorized the intrusion of criminal law into the details of marital intimacy. He declined to extend his conclusions (at least on that occasion) to the manufacture or distribution of contraceptives, or to fornication, adultery, homosexuality, and abortion—that is, to extend them outside the precise precincts of the marital bedroom.

Roe v. *Wade:* What Went Wrong

Contraception is an easy case, and when, four years later, in *Griswold* v. *Connecticut,* the Court adopted much of Harlan's dissent and struck down the Connecticut statute, no one but the academics took much notice. Abortion was and is the signal issue, and *Roe* the crucial case. Though the energy marshaled against *Roe* came from many quarters, the briefs and argument I submitted in 1985 and again in 1989 urging the overruling of *Roe* made only the point that *Roe* was a serious misuse of the Supreme Court's authority. *Roe* was a prime example of twisted judging. But I also believed that the right to privacy was a correct conclusion from good judicial reasoning. And when the Bush administration called me back to argue a *Roe* follow-on, *Webster* v. *Reproductive Health Services,*[6] I got to say so with unmistakable emphasis. This is how I began:

> Today the United States asks this Court to reconsider and overrule its decision in *Roe* v. *Wade.* At the outset, I

would like to make quite clear how limited that submission is. First, we are not asking the Court to unravel the fabric of unenumerated and privacy rights which this Court has woven. . . . Rather, we are asking the Court to pull this one thread. . . .[7]

My line was consistent with *Poe*, which I embraced as correct in the government's briefs and argument. Harlan had explicitly declined to extend his argument to abortion. But just as the framers of a constitutional provision or the draftsmen of a statute may adopt a principle that outruns their specific intentions, so might a court precedent or a judge's opinion outrun specific intentions. The reasoning, the underlying principle are more important than the specific intentions of the author. What needs to be shown is that *Roe* is different from *Poe* in principle, whatever Justice Harlan might have said about abortion in the course of his opinion.

First, *Poe* was a criminal case where the statute directed inquiry into the details of marital intimacy. It would not be illogical to strike down the Connecticut contraceptive-use statute but to tolerate the regulation, say, of distribution. An inconsistency appears only if you assume that the reason for the constitutional judgment on the first is that there is a constitutional right to contracepted intercourse generally. Harlan did not proclaim such a general constitutional right. He stood on the firmer but narrower principle that there is a right to carry on such relations free of inquiry. There is nothing illogical about saying that, though the state may take an interest in and seek to discourage some things, it may nonetheless not inquire into them coercively.

A later case, *Eisenstadt* v. *Baird*[8] (1972), struck down a statute forbidding the distribution of contraceptives to unmarried persons. Justice Brennan's opinion for the Court declined to identify a fundamental right to obtain contraceptives, and thus coyly denied going beyond *Griswold.* Brennan said the statute, forbidding distribution only to unmarried persons, was a denial "of the equal protection of the laws." He did, however, make this passing remark: "If the right of privacy means anything, it is the right of the *individual,* married or single, to be free from unwarranted governmental intrusion into matters so fundamentally affecting the person as the decision whether to bear or beget a child."[9] Thus was the seed planted from which *Roe* grew, so that later, in 1977, Justice Brennan could say that what *Griswold* stood for all along was the proposition that there is a "constitutional protection of individual autonomy in matters of childbearing."[10]

The second, more important, distinction between *Roe* and *Poe* rests on the fact that "abortion is different. It involves the purposeful termination . . . of potential life. And . . . in the minds of many legislators who pass abortion regulation, it is not merely potential but actual human life."[11] Those who press for and pass legislation limiting access to abortion are convinced that abortion ends an innocent human life, so that, whatever else is involved, it is not a matter of privacy. So, when Justice Brennan, in *Baird,* a contraception case, slipped in the irrelevant term "childbearing," he was digging a kind of surreptitious doctrinal tunnel to get from *Poe* to *Roe,* a tunnel that a year later would allow Justice Blackmun to get past the critical barrier between contraception and abortion, between what undoubtedly is a matter of privacy and what to some is murder.

The Constitution has no language speaking directly to the right of privacy, yet I believe the proper use of judicial method allows the inference to such a right. If the Constitution implied that a nonviable[12] fetus is a person entitled to equal protection of the laws, then laws restricting abortion would be constitutionally compelled.[13] I know no argument forcing that inference, but I also know of no argument that the nonviable fetus is *not* such a person. On this question the Constitution is silent. It is in that space that legislators must choose. It is an utter non sequitur to pass from the premise that the Constitution is silent on this point to the conclusion that legislation must assume that the fetus is *not* a person. Nor is it sensible or even logical to argue that the very importance of the question forces us to fill up society's answer in constitutional rather than legislative terms. Matters of war and peace, the choice between socialism and capitalism, whether there shall be race and gender discrimination in private employment, are just some of the questions of equal importance; they too are decided not in constitutional but in legislative terms.[14]

That the Constitution leaves the status of the fetus open is not only a rational position; it responds to the energy behind the abortion debate. *Brown* may have outraged many people, but too many of those who were outraged did not like black people. In the end, this was an ugly motivation, which our constitutional system was right to exclude from consideration. But no such dispositions, fundamentally at war with the principles of fairness, of liberty, and of equal treatment under law, animate the legislation limiting the right to an abortion. On the contrary. It is in part because Justice Blackmun's opinion in *Roe*—or any opinion that could have been written—so failed to meet the moral urgency of this position that it has consistently evoked such outrage.

The moral inadequacy of the *Roe* opinion is matched by its inadequacy as a piece of legal reasoning supposed to justify a major and controversial constitutional innovation.

Justice Blackmun begins by rehearsing the history of abortion and of its regulation, beginning with the Persian Empire. What is remarkable about this lengthy recital is that it proves nothing at all, and Justice Blackmun hardly suggests that it does. It merely shows that convictions about abortion have varied a great deal, although they have tended to be rather more against than for. Nor is there even any discernible trend pointing in the direction he wants to travel.[15] On the contrary, Justice Blackmun's account shows that at about the time when the Fourteenth Amendment was adopted there was a notable increase in the stringency of antiabortion laws.[16] And, more remarkably still, he does not (because he cannot[17]) give a single example of another nation with abortion laws as permissive as the limits he is about to impose on all American legislation.[18] This radical adventuresomeness of *Roe* is in itself sufficient to distinguish it from *Poe* and *Griswold*. *Griswold*, after all, struck down a statute unique and anachronistic in American jurisprudence. Justice Blackmun, who had set out the relevant materials in great detail, did not even seem to notice this fact.

Equally remarkable is the aphoristic acknowledgment of the principal objection to what the Court was about to announce:

> The pregnant woman cannot be isolated in her privacy. She carries an embryo and, later, a fetus. . . . The situation therefore is inherently different from marital intimacy . . . or marriage, or procreation, or education, with which [the Court's prior decisions were] concerned. . . . It is reasonable and appropriate for a State to decide that at some point in time another interest, that of . . . potential human life, becomes significantly involved. The woman's privacy is no longer sole and any right of privacy she possesses must be measured accordingly.[19]

Yet the closest Justice Blackmun comes to proposing a response to this dilemma is his trimester formulation: in the first trimester there may be no restriction on a medically competent decision to terminate the pregnancy; in the second trimester (because now it is no longer the case that abortion has a lesser incidence of medical risk than carrying the pregnancy to term) there may be regulation in the interests of the mother's health; and in the final trimester—when the fetus is viable—abortions may be restricted to cases where the mother's health is in danger. There is no doubt that the passage of time is believed by many to make the case for abortion more troublesome, and regulation in many Western nations makes such distinctions (though none are so permissive as *Roe*).[20]

What Justice Blackmun ordains would have some plausibility as a legislative resolution of the dilemma, but of course this is not supposed to be a legislative resolution. The Court has no warrant to write one. *Roe* is supposed to be a decision in principle, explaining fundamental, constitutional, and therefore principled constraints on what real legislatures decide. And as such the decision is a relentless series of non sequiturs and ipse dixits. For instance, one wonders why, as a matter of constitutional principle, the state's interest in protecting the fetus becomes strong enough to force a woman to carry it to term, overriding her wish to be rid of it,[21] just at a stage defined by the fact that the fetus might possibly survive outside the mother.

Justice Blackmun was evidently moved by the truly horrible spectacle of women—especially poor and ignorant women—suffering mutilation and death in desperate attempts to end unwanted pregnancies. The majority must have felt this was too grave a social ill to await either the changes that were occurring in many state legislatures or the formulation of a more satisfactory constitutional rationale. And it is this conviction of moral goodness that surely must have contributed to the majority's ferocious protectiveness of its handiwork—while the majority supporting *Roe* was dwindling within, and a contrary line of abortion-funding decisions had opened up without. But it is exactly this conviction of moral rectitude unmatched by any convincing logic that is infuriating—and that distinguished *Roe* from *Brown,* whose moral principle, after all, is broad and simple and clear, and *Miranda,* which, though legislative in much the way *Roe* is, has come to be accepted as useful by most modern police departments.

Giving Reason a Bad Name

One of the worst effects of *Roe* was that it gave legal reasoning a bad name. It is no surprise, then, that many turned for relief to the apparent security of Judge Bork's doctrine of original intent. The flight from reason to mechanical rules that promise relief from the necessities of judgment shows up in Justice White's stunningly harsh and dismissive opinion in *Bowers* v. *Hardwick*[22] (1986), the homosexual-sodomy case.

Bowers upheld a Georgia criminal statute punishing adult, consensual homosexual sodomy, against a challenge invoking the constitutional right of privacy.[23] Justice White first emphasized that "sodomy was a criminal offense at common law and was forbidden by the law of the original thirteen States when they ratified the Bill of Rights. In 1868, when the Fourteenth Amendment was ratified, all but 5 of the 37 States in the Union had criminal sodomy laws."[24] This kind of gross historical enumeration is not even conclusive in giving the best interpretation of the original meaning of a broad general principle, as *Brown* v. *Board* shows. Justice White went on to consider what the Court's jurisprudence clearly requires, that some principles of growth and development must be acknowledged, but concluded that:

> until 1961, all 50 States outlawed sodomy, and today, 24 States and the District of Columbia continue to provide criminal penalties for sodomy performed in private and between consenting adults. Against this background, to claim that the right to engage in such conduct is "deeply rooted in this Nation's history and tradition" or "implicit in the concept of ordered liberty" is, at best, facetious.[25]

Here Justice White invokes practices and understandings to preclude reasoning, not to assist it. Unless one takes the implausible line that people generally choose their sexual orientation, then to criminalize any enjoyment of their sexual powers by a whole category of persons is either an imposition of very great cruelty or an exercise in hypocrisy inviting arbitrary and abusive applications of the criminal law. *Poe* and *Griswold* did emphasize the sanctity of marital intimacy, so that a step beyond those cases would have had to be taken to reach the conclusion Justice Blackmun urged in a particularly moving dissent. But it is a short step, and one authorized by reason and tradition: Hardwick was threatened with prosecution for having consensual sex with another man behind a closed bedroom door in his own home. The police found out about it by an uninvited accident. Here the conduct was truly private. It concerned no one else except in the question-begging sense that some may be offended by the very knowledge that such conduct goes unpunished. What is left is an act of private association and communication. The fact that sexuality is implicated seems an anatomical irrelevance.

There is, to be sure, at least as widespread conviction about the immorality of homosexual activity as there is condemnation of abortion. And evidence that the level of homosexuality varies widely among cultures suggests that social pressures may have some effect in influencing even individual orientation. So various forms of condemnation may not just be purposelessly cruel but, rather, manifestations of society's concern to influence the deepest elements of its culture and structure: family stability and a climate of self-discipline. Yet I believe Justice White's extrapolation from his objection to *Roe* was incorrect.

The constitutional problem with abortion turns on whether the life of an innocent person is at stake. In the case of homosexuality, the most that can be said is that society must be allowed some scope to shape its culture, to influence what kind of society it will be: educating children and defining family structures are among the most pervasive and longstanding examples. So in *Harris* v. *McRae,* the abortion-funding case, the Court said that a government, though it may not criminalize abortion, may express its disapproval of abortions by refusing to pay for them. An analogous authority is claimed when governments decline to hire those whose commitments or ways of life it disapproves of.[26] When organized society expresses a strong judgment of value, this cannot help putting pressure on those who disagree. And it is the function of legal doctrine to develop the lines separating the right of individuals to ignore organized society's value judgments from the right of society to make and give life to such judgments. A first cut draws that line between the absolute prohibitions of the criminal law and situations where the government manages its own affairs or confers benefits. But that distinction is only a beginning: some benefits are so general and essential that withholding them may put as much pressure on individuals as the threat of prison. Legal reasoning will recognize this and work out a further system of distinctions.

What would be unreasonable would be to insist that any pressure from government is allowable only if it can pass the same constitutional test as the final pressure of the criminal law. Such extremism is the mirror image of the illiberal position that sees individuals as totally the creatures of the state, so that all state actions must pass the same constitutional test.[27] A more pluralistic vision values slippage between what the state wants and how individuals make their lives. The evolving doctrines of constitutional liberty are a way of keeping the two from getting too close, while allowing each to exist. In the end, what is important is that the majority be able to take substantial steps toward fashioning the kind of community it wants, without making it impossible for dissenters and nonconformists to make their own lives while living in the same cities and nation.

The Bush administration invited me back to present its argument for overruling *Roe* in a friend-of-the-Court argument in *Webster* v. *Reproductive Health Services*. I judged that this was a unique occasion on which to accomplish two things: to remove—from the campaign to re-establish the law in general and the effort to overrule *Roe* in particular—the albatross of originalist rigorism; and to clarify that overruling *Roe* would not slam the Court door to any complaints in the future about excesses in abortion regulation.[28] This I asserted at the very outset of my argument. The second point emerged in a colloquy with Justice O'Connor:

> Justice O'Connor: Do you say there is no fundamental right to decide whether or not? . . . to procreate?
>
> **A:** I would hesitate to formulate the right in such abstract terms, and I think the Court prior to *Roe versus Wade* quite prudently also avoided such sweeping generalities. That was the wisdom of *Griswold*.
>
> Justice O'Connor: Do you think that the state has the right to, if in a future century we had a serious overpopulation problem, has a right to require women to have abortions after so many children?

A: I surely do not. That would be quite a different matter.

Justice O'Connor: What do you rest that on?

A: Because unlike abortion, which involves the purposeful termination of future life, that would involve not preventing an operation, but violently . . . laying hands on a woman and submitting her to an operation. . . .

Justice O'Connor: And you would rest that on substantive due-process protection?

A: Absolutely.

Justice Kennedy: How do you define the liberty interest of the woman in that connection?

A: The liberty interest against a seizure would be concerned. That is how the Court analyzed the matter in *Griswold.*[29] That is how Justice Harlan analyzed the matter in *Poe versus Ullman* which is, in some sense, the root of this area of law. . . .

Justice Kennedy: How would you define the . . . liberty interest . . . of a woman in an abortion case?

A: I would define it in terms of the concrete impositions on the woman which so offended the Court in *Griswold* and which are not present in the *Roe* situation.

The point was elliptical, as it had to be in the course of a ten-minute argument. But I hope it planted the seeds for important distinctions. There are several ways a state might enforce its population policy. It might forcibly submit women to abortions; or it might simply deny welfare benefits to third and subsequent children, on an analogy to the abortion-funding cases. In drawing attention to the violence of the intrusion in the first way, I sought to bring the abortion issue back to the particularity of the *Poe* decision, where the type and circumstances of the intrusion put it at odds with the Constitution in a number of convergent ways. The denial of funding, by contrast, asked the question in the most abstract, unanchored, and therefore inappropriate terms. And a statute in Justice O'Connor's hypothetical future which kept a woman in jail until she agreed to abort her third child, or punished her for not aborting it, would be more like the first, the bloodthirsty alternative.

By the same token, having one day abandoned *Roe,* the Court may reasonably distinguish between statutes forbidding abortions outright and statutes requiring a delay of a few days in which a woman may consider alternatives to abortion, which the clinic is obliged to tell her about; or between statutes regulating abortion services and statutes punishing women who undergo abortions. This last is a distinction that might have considerable practical importance with the greater availability of safe, simple, self-administered pharmaceuticals to induce early-term abortions. In fact, medical discoveries might then make this whole constitutional episode moot.

Abortion has been unlike any other Supreme Court issue in the heat it has generated. It has distorted the Supreme Court's own jurisprudence. As Justice O'Connor has said, "The . . . normal rules of law, procedure and constitutional adjudication suddenly become irrelevant because a case touches on the subject of abortion."[30] Abortion has distorted the public's attitudes and expectations regarding the Supreme Court, dominating public and political debates that should have had a wider and thus more illuminating focus. And the Reagan administration's apparent obsession with this subject distracted attention from what I conceive to have been its real project: restoring reasonableness and responsibility to the practice of judging. As a result of this one issue, a sense of irreconcilable polarization hung over our initiatives, not just in this area but also in other areas, such as race and the separation of powers.

4

RACE

*Distinctions between citizens solely because
of their ancestry are odious to a free
people whose institutions are founded on
the doctrine of equality.[1]*

*Racial discrimination in any form and in
any degree has no justifiable part
whatever in our democratic way of life.[2]*

*A*fter three centuries of slavery and another hundred years of apartheid, neither *Brown* v. *Board* nor the Civil Rights Acts of the 1960s had closed the dreadful gap between the life situations of blacks and whites.[3] Many liberals and civil-rights activists are convinced that banning discrimination is not enough. They have pushed everywhere for preference for blacks. Government should set targets—quotas—in its own employment and contracting; private employers and institutions must have these targets forced on them if they do not take them up on their own. All this is urged under the banner of affirmative action.[4] I believe this conception of affirmative action dangerously aggrandizes government. It is a threat to liberty and to the basic right of every person to be considered as a distinct individual and not in terms of the groups to which government says he belongs. The Reagan administration was committed to ending the drift to a quota society and to dismantling government-imposed racial preferences. The courts and especially the Supreme Court were where this battle was fought, so for four years it was my struggle. By 1989 we had come a long way toward setting things right. Along the way I had to contend with some of my allies, who were committed to the same project but had a different, perhaps more rigorous logic. Logic aside, some have described the new clarity in the Supreme Court's approach to race, a clarity we called for during eight years, as the "legal lynching of Black America's hope."[5]

Civil Rights Before Reagan

The Civil War Amendments and the Reconstruction-era civil-rights acts abolished slavery and were supposed to remove race-based legal disabilities, but blacks were not equal before the law until 1954, when, in *Brown* v. *Board* and its progeny,[6] the Supreme Court made clear that state segregation, by way of the separate-but-equal sophism, was constitutionally forbidden. But this was not enough. The Constitution guarantees all persons the equal protection of the laws, and *Brown* did not touch discrimination in private housing, business opportunities, private education, transport and accommodations, and, most important, private employment. For blacks finally to enjoy real equality, private as well as government racism had to be rooted out, and under Hubert Humphrey's leadership this was the simple purpose of the Civil Rights Act of 1964.[7]

Opposition to the employment component of the 1964 Act (Title VII) was not limited to racists. Many, like Senator Dirksen, accepted the antidiscrimination principle but worried that "federal bureaucrats" would use their enforcement powers to impose racial quotas and preferences wherever a work force was not statistically "balanced."[8] Humphrey rebutted this charge, saying that his bill provided no more than that "race shall not be a basis for making personnel decisions," and called the quota-hiring fear a "nonexistent . . . bugaboo." To make good on this reassurance, he agreed to add a clause stating that nothing in the act "shall be interpreted to require . . . grant[ing] preferential treatment . . . because of . . . race . . . or on account of an imbalance which may exist with respect to the total number or percentage of persons of any race . . . employed. . . ."[9] As much as anything, this took the wind out of his opponents' sails; and the law was enacted.[10] Where federal bureaucrats, liberal judges, and civil-rights activists tried—with some success—to take this law proved how reasonable Senator Dirksen's fears had been and how empty Hubert Humphrey's reassurance.

Affirmative action was the issue. The Act literally outlawed employment decisions made on the basis of race or gender, protecting everyone, white or black, man or woman. But of course the many preferential programs adopted by employers all over the country to increase minority representation did just that: they made decisions on the basis of race. Taking the Act at its word, Brian Weber sued Kaiser Steel and its union because as a white he had been denied admission to a training program that, in accordance with the company and union's affirmative-action plan, reserved one-half of the places for blacks. Justice Brennan's opinion for a 5–2 Court in *United Steelworkers* v. *Weber*[11] may well stand as the masterpiece of his particular skill in advancing his policy agenda:

> [Although we concede that the white plaintiff's argument, based on a] literal interpretation of . . . the Act [, which makes it] unlawful to "discriminate . . . because . . . of race" . . . is not without force, . . . it would be ironic indeed if a law triggered by a Nation's concern over centuries of racial injustice and intended to improve the lot of those who had "been excluded from the American dream for so long," 110 Cong. Rec. 6552 (remarks of Senator Humphrey), constituted the first legislative prohibition of all voluntary, private, race-conscious efforts to abolish traditional patterns of racial segregation and hierarchy.[12]

Justice Rehnquist called Justice Brennan's way with the statute here "reminiscent not of jurists such as Hale, Holmes, and Hughes, but of escape artists such as Houdini." But there was common sense behind Brennan's opinion. He was able to invoke management prerogatives and a distaste for government regulation, values that did not often move him, in order to get and hold his majority:

Title VII could not have been enacted into law without substantial support from legislators in both Houses who traditionally resisted federal regulation of private business. Those legislators demanded as a price for their support that "management prerogatives, and union freedoms . . . be left undisturbed to the greatest extent possible." . . . Clearly, a prohibition against all voluntary, race-conscious affirmative action would disserve these ends. Such a prohibition would augment the powers of the Federal Government and diminish traditional management prerogatives while at the same time impeding attainment of the ultimate statutory goals.

The upshot was that private employers were free to experiment with ways of increasing opportunities for minority workers. This may not have been what the Act had in mind, but in itself it seems a sensible enough result.

However, as Justice Brennan knew, the *Weber* case did not stand alone. In 1971 the Supreme Court, in *Griggs* v. *Duke Power Co.*,[13] had greatly expanded the exposure of employers to Title VII lawsuits by minority workers. The Act clearly meant to catch the employer who discriminated intentionally. But the Court went further. It said that an employer might be liable even if no open or hidden discrimination were charged. So long as it was shown that the way the employer recruited his employees or ran his business had the effect of keeping the numbers of minority workers below some assumed correct proportion—so long as the employer's practices had what was called a "disparate impact" on minority employment—the employer had to come forward to explain how his practices were justified by "business necessity." If his explanation was not to a court's or bureaucrat's satisfaction, he could be subject to ruinous liability.

The *Griggs* case did expose a problem: intentional discrimination is hard to prove. In *Griggs* itself, the Duke Power Company, which had openly excluded blacks from all but the most menial jobs, responded to the 1964 Act by imposing a high-school-diploma requirement for the more desirable job categories. Given North Carolina's history of segregation, the new requirement eliminated almost all black applicants. This sort of restriction was a frequent barrier to economic progress by blacks.[14] It would have been easy and traditional for a trial court to have simply found that standing unexplained, Duke's behavior was sufficient indirect evidence of discriminatory intent—that the scheme was just a pretext for discrimination.[15] But there are more difficult cases, where an employer or union innocently but heedlessly puts up a barrier to minority opportunity. For example, it was the practice of many craft unions to limit admission to their apprenticeship programs (and thus to the craft) to children of union members. Trivial or pointless or obsolete barriers should not protect employers from liability any more than the kind of pretext we saw in *Griggs*. Chief Justice Burger approached this problem in very general terms, speaking of practices "fair in form but discriminatory in operation." Such language was coupled with what may have seemed like a willingness to let the disappointed worker base his case on little more than a showing of a racially unbalanced work force, making the employer show in his defense something as tough as that the practice was necessary to his business.

Of course the facts in *Griggs* were awful, and for some reason the lower courts had not found the whole arrangement a transparent sham, as they well might have. But hard cases make bad laws; many employers, federal enforcement officials, and lower courts understood *Griggs* as a mandate for quota hiring. After all, any large employer must operate according to some routines, and if at the end of the day the numbers do not come out "right," it is easy to charge that something in these routines must be working as a "barrier" to equal opportunity. Then it would be up to a federal bureaucrat or judge to decide whether the challenged practice was nevertheless justified. These officials would determine whether the employer's own conception of his business was correct, and whether a particular requirement was "necessary" to do the job. For example, imagine a research-oriented university that requires a Ph.D. of all of its teaching faculty, because it thinks of itself as a certain kind of community of scholars. If such a requirement operated to limit opportunities for blacks, as it likely would, it would be up to federal officials of dubious qualifications to decide whether this is what teaching at a university should be and whether a Ph.D. is "necessary" to teach there.

Although Chief Justice Burger may not have grasped the practical implications of the phrases that rolled off his pen, many others did. Some applauded the fact that in only a few years the march of events seemed to have made the Act powerful enough to compel the kind of compensatory justice they had felt was needed all along but knew they could not have asked for openly in 1964. When this is combined with *Weber*'s open invitation to employers to engage in reverse discrimination without fear of lawsuits by whites, it is no surprise that one expert commission concluded that federal policies were "those that would be adopted if the desired effect were to force employers to a quota system to achieve a representative work force."[16]

The Supreme Court, however, was having second thoughts. In one case, the New York City Transit Authority would not employ anyone using narcotic drugs (including persons in methadone maintenance programs). The federal courts in New York found that this rule was racially discriminatory because it excluded so many blacks and Hispanics. The Supreme Court disagreed.[17] And in *Washington* v. *Davis*,[18] the Court upheld against an equal protection challenge a verbal aptitude test used by the D.C. Police Department. With only Justices Brennan and Marshall dissenting, the Court said that "a law, neutral on its face and serving ends otherwise within the power of government to pursue, is [not] invalid under the Equal Protection Clause simply because it may affect a greater proportion of one race than of another." This, of course, was just the opposite of the point some had hoped had been established in *Griggs*.

Griggs provided some lower federal courts with a basis for treating the Civil Rights Act as a piece of radical social engineering serving the left-liberal goal of equality of result. But in the Supreme Court's treatment of affirmative action an important gap had opened up between the Constitution and the Act. The Court was changing.

The turning point was the 1978 *Bakke* case.[19] *Bakke* considered a challenge to a California state medical school that gave an absolute preference to blacks, Chicanos, Asians, and Native Americans in the competition for a limited number of places in the entering class.[20] The ruling in *Bakke* spelled real trouble for racial preferences, though at the time those committed to preferential affirmative action chose to describe the result as a victory.

Justice Brennan, writing for himself and Justices White, Marshall, and Blackmun, took a strong line. "Societal discrimination" was sufficient to justify a fixed quota, because the Constitution does not preclude all uses of race in governmental distinctions, only such "racial classifications that stigmatize—because they are drawn on the presumption that one race is inferior. . . ." But this view did not command a majority. Four Justices thought the California plan violated a federal statute, and therefore they did not reach the constitutional question. The ninth, Justice Powell, reached the constitutional question and rejected Justice Brennan's constitutional standard. He thought that the rigid quota, which set aside a fixed number of places for minority applicants, was unconstitutional, and therefore struck down that part of the plan:

> Petitioner urges us to . . . hold for the first time that discrimination against members of the white "majority" cannot be suspect if its purpose can be characterized as "benign." . . . It is far too late to argue that the guarantee of equal protection to *all* persons permits the recognition of special wards entitled to a degree of protection greater than that accorded others.
>
> . . . Preferring members of any one group for no reason other than race or ethnic origin is discrimination for its own sake. This the Constitution forbids. . . . Brown v. Board of Education, 347 U.S. 483 (1954). The State certainly has a legitimate and substantial interest in ameliorating, or eliminating where feasible, the dis-

abling effects of identified discrimination. . . . That goal [is] far more focused than the remedying of the effects of "societal discrimination," an amorphous concept of injury that may be ageless in its reach into the past.

This was the language that the enthusiasts of preferences chose to overlook in analyzing *Bakke*. Instead, they focused on the fact that Justice Powell permitted the use of race as a factor in the medical school's admission process—but only because *Bakke* involved a university academic program. Justice Powell emphasized that for him this implicated the competing First Amendment value of academic freedom, the freedom of a university to manage itself and define its own goals.[21] But proponents of preferences chose to overlook the fact that such constitutionally grounded qualifications are absent in most other cases, and to see instead in Powell's opinion something like the general celebration of preferences found in Justice Brennan's and Justice Marshall's dissents. Powell's scruples seemed so nice that politicians and the public generally concluded that, though this case was lost in part, affirmative action in general had squeaked by—as it did the next year, in a different statutory context, in the *Weber* case.

Employers who had reason to fear the *Griggs* overhang welcomed *Weber*. If your work force is not racially balanced, you may get sued (*Griggs*). If you use quotas and preferences to make the numbers come out right, you are in the clear (*Weber*). Where *Bakke* fit in was not yet apparent.

The Carter administration had defended affirmative action before the Supreme Court in *Weber* and *Bakke*. It gave preference to blacks and women in judgeships, presidential appointments, civil-service jobs, and government grants and contracts.[22] And the mood had spread to state and local governments, private businesses, universities, and hospitals.

A New Turn: Color-Blindness

A decade of aggressive affirmative action had in some ways made us a better country. Blacks and women found places in businesses and institutions, sometimes in significant numbers, often for the first time. In a society that had practiced public and private apartheid, the presence of those who had previously been excluded was an earnest on a commitment to a nation of individual opportunity without arbitrary barriers to individual aspiration and achievement. But there was a sinister side to the growth in preferences. White males increasingly resented that their share of a shrinking pie was decreasing. In the Carter years they increasingly believed they were being leapfrogged for jobs and places in college by persons who (in accordance with the objective measures we had become used to) were less qualified. And though our system of rewarding ability and effort had always been imperfect, never before had the losers been asked to celebrate their losses, to feel guilty about wanting to win in a fair contest.[23]

In addition, those who benefited from the racial preferences felt a strange ambiguity: it put their teeth on edge that they could not quite say to themselves that they had made it on their own.[24] If they admitted that they had been preferred, their response was often truculence, or self-doubt, or an elaborate sense of obligation to their communities, which, though admirable, was not quite freely chosen.

This ambivalence led to evasion and dishonesty. It became fashionable to make up all kinds of fancy stories about how perfectly reasonable measures of ability and achievement were somehow unfair and bigoted.[25] It seemed that we were ready to cheat on standards of excellence or even competence in order to avoid facing the fact that centuries of deprivation had left many blacks less qualified than whites.

To me the most disturbing aspect of this system of preferences was the pervasive bureaucratization and politicization it involved[26]—as Senator Dirksen had anticipated in 1964, before Hubert Humphrey soothed away his fears. Enforcing preferences—directly or indirectly through the *Griggs* business-necessity test—gave the government a hold on parts of private institutions that had previously eluded its grasp. The politicization was just as sinister. If jobs were handed out according to membership in a group that has managed to attract political power, then the private sector and private institutions are not responsible to themselves or to the market, but to politics. If the job market is thus distorted, not only do employers have to play a political game in order to get employees, but also people seeking jobs do so through politics, not their own capabilities.

And the supposed benefits of the system were far from clear. It was obvious that preferences were irrelevant to the deplorable plight of the black under-class. Preferences tend to help the black middle class and the most ambitious and ablest poor blacks—

people who would not in any event sink into the ghettos of despair.[27]

Just as quotas and preferences had become a gut commitment uniting the attitudes and principles of left-collectivism, so they focused the opposition of the rising conservative and libertarian tide. The racial policies of the Carter years were made an explicit target of the Reagan campaign, and this helped attract many of the traditional Democrats who supported Reagan.[28]

The motto that announced the new policy was "color-blindness." This was a term drawn from the first Justice Harlan's* dissent in *Plessy* v. *Ferguson,* the 1896 decision upholding the constitutionality of a Louisiana law requiring "separate but equal accommodations" for "white and colored" railway passengers:

> The white race deems itself to be the dominant race in this country. And so it is, in prestige, in achievements, in education, in wealth, and in power. So, I doubt not, it will continue to be for all time, if it remains true to its great heritage and holds fast to the principles of constitutional liberty. But in view of the Constitution, in the eye of the law, there is in this country no superior, dominant, ruling class of citizens. There is no caste here. Our Constitution is color-blind, and neither knows nor tolerates classes among citizens.[29]

Aside from the white-supremacist caveats, Harlan's dissent offered a pretty good slogan for this part of the Reagan Revolution.

* John Marshall Harlan, grandfather of the Justice by the same name who wrote the *Poe* dissent and for whom I clerked in 1960–61.

False Notes: *Bob Jones* and Voting Rights

Color-blindness was fine in theory, but in practice the policy got off to a bad start. In the first years, before the midterm election of 1982, the administration embarked on two spectacularly misconceived projects—the *Bob Jones* case[30] and the opposition to extension of the Voting Rights Act.

In addition to conservatives and old-style liberals, there were also some drawn to Reagan by less idealistic motives. The South had in many ways become a less segregated society than some parts of the North, and black voters in the South held the balance of power and used it skillfully.[31] Some Southerners never completely accepted this passing of the old, segregated order, and they too became part of the remarkable 1980 Republican sweep of the South. The currents of their influence also flowed into what was to become the Reagan civil-rights agenda.

Bob Jones, a fundamentalist Christian university in Greenville, South Carolina, had first opened its doors to unmarried blacks in 1975, but enforced a rule against interracial dating, which it believed violated biblical norms. Nonprofit educational institutions enjoy federal tax exemptions. The IRS had ruled, however, that this statutory exemption for charitable purposes was subject to an implicit condition that the charitable deduction not be used in a way that violates "public policy." Racial segregation was such a violation. This ruling was particularly important in clipping the wings of the private, all-white "academies" that had sprung up to avoid school desegregation after the *Brown* decision. Bob Jones University— where there were black students—did not quite violate the purpose or even the wording of the IRS policy. Nonetheless, during the Carter years the IRS had denied Bob Jones its tax deduction because of its interracial-dating rule. The case was before the Supreme Court on the university's objection.

Until 1981 the Justice Department and Solicitor General defended the IRS, the "client" agency, but then there was a change of direction, perhaps precipitated by a letter in late 1981 from Mississippi Congressman Trent Lott to Deputy Attorney General Edward Schmults.[32] The Department's new opposition to the IRS policy before the Supreme Court was not without technical merit; there is something troublesome about having the bureaucrats in the IRS make social policy. And the fact that Bob Jones's policy was only tangential to the central problem of the segregated academies made the IRS ruling seem unnecessarily intrusive. But these technical arguments were completely swamped by what seemed like the administration's abandonment of a longstanding federal commitment to desegregation. As the opening move in the administration's civil-rights policy, the decision to support blatantly racist if somewhat nutty practices displayed—if nothing else—a lack of strategic insight and a complete miscalculation of the civil-rights community's strength and determination. In any event, the Department's position was rejected with only one dissent in the Supreme Court. The episode was viewed by many as though it were the thirteenth chime of the clock—casting doubt on the sincerity of the administration's "color-blind" civil-rights policy or, worse, investing the term with a meaning that drove away many of its natural allies.

The damage from *Bob Jones* was compounded by

the mishandling of the voting-rights dispute in 1982. The Voting Rights Act of 1965 attacked the many tricks used to discourage or dilute the impact of black voting: literacy tests, complex and inconvenient registration requirements, gerrymandered districts that submerged black voting power and guaranteed an all-white sweep. The Act was due to expire in 1982, and there was a debate about its re-enactment. In 1980 the Supreme Court had held that only arrangements that intentionally discriminated against minority voting rights violated the Act.[33] A sophisticated part of the civil-rights movement hoped that upon re-enactment the Congress would move beyond intentional discrimination to something like the *Griggs* test—leading to proportional representation of minority voters by minority candidates. Carried to its logical conclusion, this project would institutionalize racial politics, guaranteeing racially "balanced" legislatures, city councils, and school boards.

Such an effects test was the opposite of a "color-blind" civil-rights policy. Had the administration taken an early and strong lead in favor of a simple re-enactment of the 1965 Act, a color-blind antidiscrimination voting-rights act would have been within its reach. Instead, the administration lost all credibility and control over the situation by supporting the few Congressmen and Senators who opposed any extension of the Act.[34] In the end, only an ingenious compromise devised by Senators Dole and Hatch—a compromise so equivocal as to be incomprehensible—staved off the most radical proportional-representation formulation and avoided the disaster of a presidential veto and a certain subsequent override.[35] Several years later, in my first Court term as Solicitor

General, it was my unenviable task to try for a sensible construction of this language.[36]

No Middle Ground

It was at about this time, in the summer of 1982, that I became a consultant to the White House task force formulating policy on employment discrimination. I emphasized the sinister tendency toward a bureaucratic-collectivist state implicit in government-imposed racial and gender preferences. My proposals urged the government's withdrawal from the preference business, coupled with a strong antidiscriminatory enforcement policy and strong, preferential remedies when an employer had been shown to discriminate. In their reaction to my proposals I found out how deeply Brad Reynolds and Mike Horowitz felt about the concept of color-blindness. They bridled at government-imposed preferences and "race-conscious relief," even as a remedy for proven discrimination. Color-blindness for them meant that remedies for proven discrimination must either be punitive or strictly compensatory—that is, only the individuals discriminated against may be given the job they should have had, together with whatever wages they had lost during the interim. Relief, as the tag went, must be victim-specific; if so it is color-blind, for it is predicated on victim status, not race.

There is considerable force to this argument, but in practice it means that discrimination will often go unremedied, since by the time a lawsuit is done the specific victims will have scattered and there will be no one to compensate. To my mind, insisting on proven discrimination already went far enough in limiting the role of government as social engineer. Nor did it deprive competing whites of anything they would have had if there had been no wrong in the particular case. When I urged that victim specificity was an unnecessary and unacceptable addition to a sound antidiscrimination policy, my proposal met with cold contempt from Brad Reynolds and hot fury from Mike Horowitz. Mike treated me to the kind of tirade—fervent and heartfelt—for which he had become famous: deregulatory, economic-liberty concerns were beside the point; this was a moral issue; when Lincoln freed the slaves, questions of efficiency and government interference did not come into it; and where racial justice is the issue, he would not gag at any amount of government control. Racial preferences of any kind were unjust, I was told. People like me did not understand how struggling white working people were hurt and outraged to see their efforts disregarded in favor of others, who were no more deserving and had not suffered anything more or worse than they had. These were the people who had elected Ronald Reagan, not fancy-pants neocons like me.

Victim specificity was the order of the day; it was the President's policy. Three years later I was Solicitor General and it was my job to present that policy to the Supreme Court.

False Dawn: *Stotts*

Victim specificity had been the subject of a furious battle in 1983 between Brad Reynolds and Rex Lee regarding the position that Lee would take as Solicitor

General in the *Stotts* case.[37] The Nashville Fire Department had been accused of discriminating against blacks in hiring and promotion and had reached an agreement with the plaintiffs that it would stop its discrimination and also grant hiring and promotion preferences to blacks until certain percentages had been reached. The agreement was put before a court before there had been an adjudication, and that court had confirmed it.

Consent decrees had become quite common and straddled both sides of the line in *Weber*. Because this agreement was embodied in a court decree, it looked as if a court were ordering racial preferences—and doing so without having first adjudicated that there had been a substantive violation of law. And this seemed to contradict directly the assurances by the Act's sponsors that the Act would not be used to impose quotas or preferences. On the other hand, to the extent that these were *consent* decrees, they seemed closer to the voluntary affirmative action blessed in *Weber*. Thus consent decrees were a source of considerable doctrinal tension. In *Stotts* this tension surfaced in a way that was most sympathetic to the grievances of the complaining whites: layoffs were needed, so whites were losing their jobs because they were white, in order to maintain the balance previously achieved under a racially preferential affirmative action plan.

Reynolds wanted to use this case to establish the proposition that relief, even for proven violations of the Civil Rights Act, must always be victim-specific. Litigated decrees, as well as consent decrees favoring blacks or women as a group, had to go. The career lawyers in the Solicitor General's office resisted the notion that the Act had resolved the question of what kind of relief a court could order as a remedy for a proven violation. The federal Equal Employment Opportunity Commission (EEOC) also disagreed, pointing out that such a conclusion would "call into question numerous extant consent decrees and conciliation agreements. . . ."[38] In the end, Rex Lee argued Reynolds' victim-specificity position quite forcefully.

The last sentence of Section 706(g) of the Civil Rights Act, which deals with the power of courts to order remedies, says:

> No order of the court shall require the . . . reinstatement, or promotion of an individual as an employee . . . if such individual . . . was suspended or discharged for any reason other than discrimination on account of race, color, religion, sex, or national origin. . . .

On its own, this language seems to be directed at another problem identified in Justice Blackmun's *Stotts* dissent—an employer does not ever have to keep on or promote someone who is fired for a perfectly good reason. Yet the legislative history contains strong statements by authoritative spokesmen supporting a broader construction. For example, Representative Celler, principal draftsman of Section 706(g), said that "the court could not order that any preference be given to any particular race . . . , but would be limited to ordering an end to discrimination."[39] And Senator Humphrey characterized as a "nonexistent . . . bugaboo" the idea that Title VII could be used to make employees "meet a racial 'quota' or . . . achieve a certain racial balance."[40]

To take these 1964 statements at full force would have had a revolutionary effect on current practice. Courts all over the country had been imposing preferences to remedy proven discrimination, and parties had been settling suits on this basis as well, with and without the blessing of court orders.[41] That Rex Lee embraced the arguments to the contrary was, therefore, a strong statement by the administration. That Justice White, writing for the Court, appeared to accept that argument, without the tentative qualifiers in Rex's brief, was startling. He quoted Senator Humphrey's language and spoke of "the policy behind Section 706(g) . . . which is to provide make-whole relief only to those who have been actual victims of illegal discrimination."[42] It is no wonder, then, that Rex, who had argued the case and been plagued with criticism within the administration for seeming to be overly hesitant in pushing the color-blindness agenda, declared the *Stotts* decision a "slam-dunk" when it was announced on June 12, 1984.

Reynolds immediately swung into action. He gave interviews declaring final victory in the victim-specificity battle. More importantly—and disastrously—he wrote letters to all the state and local governments that had entered into preferential schemes over the years in settlement of Justice Department discrimination suits, stating that these arrangements had now been held unlawful and would have to be revised. It was soon evident that he had greatly overplayed his hand. On closer inspection the *Stotts* decision had soft spots. It was a case, after all, not about preferential hiring from a large, anonymous pool but, rather, about firing white persons with seniority and thus with settled expectations.[43]

Every lower court that considered subsequent challenges by white workers in the wake of *Stotts* concluded that the case was about something very limited—modifications of consent decrees relating to seniority systems.[44] What these lower-court judges were making of White's opinion in these subsequent decisions was fast becoming the truth about *Stotts*. Furthermore, the administration was seen as having turned sharply right in the term after *Stotts*. Ed Meese, now Attorney General, gave the agenda a harder edge. The Senate, in what was seen as a referendum on Reynolds' civil-rights policies, rejected his nomination for promotion to be Meese's Associate Attorney General.

Bear Trap

This was the state of play at the time I became Solicitor General. Reynolds felt that the lower courts were cheating him of the victory he had won in *Stotts*. He thought we would have to go back to the Supreme Court and get the Justices to say it again, and he asked me to do so in the very next case ready for Supreme Court review, *Local 28 of the Sheet Metal Workers* v. *EEOC*. This would be his vindication.

Stotts had been an unattractive case for preferential relief, involving no finding of discrimination and forcing the layoff of senior white workers. *Sheet Metal Workers* was just as unattractive a case in which to oppose preferences. The union had discriminated openly, dragged out the litigation for over twenty years, and evaded all the agreements it had made. Finally, in exasperation, a federal judge ordered a remedial regime that included a rigid numerical quota for blacks seeking to enter the trade. Despite the case's unattractiveness, the union was determined to take it to the Supreme Court, even if we did not.

The other case coming before the Court during the summer of 1985 was *Wygant* v. *Jackson Board of Education.* In a period of declining enrollment, the school board replaced its previous seniority-based layoff system with a preferential system designed to maintain as nearly as possible the ratio of minority teachers to minority students.[45] A white teacher laid off under this plan brought suit. Here was a case without any history of discrimination: a case that involved not hiring but layoffs, where the preference was designed to maintain and not just to attain racial balance. The complaint invoked the Equal Protection Clause of the Constitution against a unit of government. It did not mention Title VII. My own inclination was to press for a clear statement that the Constitution does indeed force government to be color-blind, thus trumping the doctrinal intricacies of Title VII. This did not preclude private parties from engaging in voluntary affirmative action, since private actors are not bound by the Constitution.

I felt strongly about *Wygant;* it not only posed the right question but did so on a particularly appealing set of facts. But there was no ducking *Sheet Metal Workers.* After *Stotts* I had no plausible objection to raise against making the victim-specificity argument. Victim specificity was administration policy; it had been fought out between Reynolds and Lee, and now the Supreme Court seemed to have adopted it. I was stuck.

Wygant was another matter. Sam Alito and I wrote

the brief. We spoke directly to the deepest issues at stake in the case: whether ours is to become a society defined in terms of groups; whether rights derive from group membership, or whether our society's fundamental conception is an individualistic one in which all of us ultimately stand before the law as distinct individuals. Is our Constitution in fact committed to a liberal, individualistic conception of rights and citizenship, as opposed to the collectivist vision that was becoming fashionable in academic circles under the rubrics of communitarianism and republicanism?

> As amicus curiae in *Brown* v. *Board of Education* . . . the United States argued that the Fourteenth Amendment "established the broad constitutional principle of full and complete equality of all persons under the law," and that it forbade "all distinctions based on race and color." The schoolchildren took the same position, contending that "the Fourteenth Amendment prohibits a state from making racial distinctions in the exercise of government power."[46] We make the same argument in the present case.
>
>   . . .
>
>   . . . In 1896, this Court approved the concept of "separate but equal" facilities for blacks and whites and thus upheld the arrest of Homer A. Plessy for occupying a railroad coach reserved for whites. . . . According to his petition, Plessy was seven-eighths white and one-eighth black, and "the mixture of colored blood was not discernible in him". Under Louisiana law, he was black, although in other states he apparently would have been white. Whether, if living today, he would be regarded as black or white by the Jackson Board of Education is unclear. What is clear is that his Fourteenth Amendment rights as a person were violated.

This brief drew criticism from editorialists and Supreme Court buffs for being inappropriately vivid. It was clear to me that these critics were not honest when they insisted that bureaucratic gray was the appropriate color not only for the cover, but also for the style and contents of a government brief. They would applaud vividness and passion, but only in the service of causes to which they subscribed. (That is why we had begun by quoting an earlier brief signed by Thurgood Marshall, Constance Baker Motley, and Jack Greenberg—all heroes of the civil-rights movement.)

The decision in *Wygant* came down first, in May 1986. The bottom line was ours. Wendy Wygant's firing was held to violate the Equal Protection Clause. But the opinions were equivocal and confusing. Justice Powell wrote for himself, Chief Justice Burger, and Justice Rehnquist. Powell came closer to getting it right than we had. He started from the axiom that racial classifications of any sort must meet the hardest test of constitutional justification—strict scrutiny— and that they can only pass that test if they are "narrowly tailored" to accomplish a "compelling" governmental purpose. Powell insisted that "the level of scrutiny does not change merely because the challenged classification operates against a group that historically has been subject to governmental discrimination." From that premise, Powell concluded that remedying identified instances of past discrimination was such a compelling governmental purpose as would meet strict scrutiny. On the other hand, pointing to the history of discrimination in the country or the community and to its long-term effects would not do.

Similarly, Powell rejected the argument that the school board's scheme was justified by the desire to provide role models for its minority students. "Carried to its logical extreme, the idea that black students are better off with black teachers could lead to the very system the Court rejected in *Brown* v. *Board of Education*."

Finally, Powell put the underlying moral issue at least as vividly as we had:

> . . . Justice Marshall [for the dissent] . . . sees this case not in terms of individual constitutional rights, but as an allocation of burdens "between two racial groups." . . . But the petitioners before us today are not "the white teachers as a group." They are Wendy Wygant and other individuals who claim that they were fired from their jobs because of their race. . . . The Constitution does not allocate constitutional rights to be distributed like bloc grants within discrete racial groups. . . .

Although the issue was not directly at stake, Justice Powell's opinion did state that, if the proper showing of past discrimination were made, a race-conscious remedy could extend beyond just the particular victims of the discrimination: victim specificity was rejected. Such a remedy would have to be narrowly tailored, and could not impose as heavy a burden as the Jackson layoff plan. On the other hand, the opinion also seemed to suggest that past discrimination was the only governmental interest that would justify racial preferences. That interpretation would signal a change for Justice Powell, who in *Bakke* had written that, at least in the university setting, a desire for diversity would justify taking race into account, though not to the extent of the fixed quota struck down in that case. This departure from the diversity rationale drew a sharp dissent from Justice Stevens.

As satisfying as Justice Powell's opinion was, it was not the opinion of the Court. Justice O'Connor wrote separately and at length, agreeing with Powell in large part, but worrying about the burden of self-accusation that public employers who were seeking to remedy their own past deficiencies might have to assume in order to meet Justice Powell's strictures. And Justice White, the author of *Stotts*, joined in the result on the laconic, baffling, and dyspeptic ground that, "Whatever the legitimacy of hiring goals or quotas may be, the discharge of white teachers to make room for blacks, none of whom has been shown to be a victim of racial discrimination, is quite a different matter." The Court was obviously unsettled on this issue, and unable to make clear law. I cannot help thinking that the emphasis the administration had given to this issue as *its* issue may have made at least Justices O'Connor and White hesitant about seeming to "sign on."

Wygant was a victory for what I believed in, although an equivocal one. The decision in *Sheet Metal Workers* in July was a defeat that some commentators trumpeted as final and crushing. The court-imposed quota plan in *Sheet Metal Workers* was approved by the Court on a 5–4 vote. Justice Brennan announced the judgment, but could not muster a majority for his opinion, any more than Justice Powell had been able to in *Wygant*. Brennan's opinion roundly affirmed that a limitation to victim-specific relief was required neither by the statute, nor by its legislative history, nor by the Constitution, and he went out of his way to

scold the Solicitor General for saying the contrary:
"This reading twists the plain language of the statute."
Justice Brennan ignored the fact that these very
contentions were not deployed for the first time by
me as the Reagan administration's Solicitor General,
but had been used, as Justice O'Connor pointed out
in her separate opinion, by the Court itself in *Stotts*—
with Justice Brennan in dissent.

The bottom line of this case *was* the story, and the
media declared that the Reagan administration's policy on affirmative action had been definitively and
harshly rejected by the Supreme Court. Herman
Schwartz, writing in the *Michigan Law Review*, titled
his analysis "The 1986 and 1987 Affirmative Action
Cases: It's All Over but the Shouting."[47] The details
of the *Sheet Metal Workers* opinion were swamped in
the rush to believe that we had been thoroughly
trounced: Justice Brennan could not muster a majority for his opinion. Justice Powell, who had joined the
majority in *Stotts*, went along with the result here but
wrote separately. Justice White, the author of *Stotts*,
wrote that this "may . . . be . . . one of those unusual
cases . . . [where] the general policy under Title VII
. . . to limit relief . . . to actual victims of discrimination does not apply," though he dissented because he
found the lower court's rigid quota "excessive." And
Justice Brennan himself had to emphasize the extreme nature of the facts in this case in order to
accomplish what he did: preferences may be the only
way to bring to heel an employer or a union like this
one, who "has engaged in particularly longstanding
or egregious discrimination."

On the evening of the decision I appeared on
"MacNeil, Lehrer" with a gloating Eleanor Holmes

Norton, who had been President Carter's EEOC Chairman. I said that, while we had urged that racial preferences may never be used, the Court had responded, "Not never, but hardly ever." I would have been allowed to commit hara-kiri on camera, but my cheerful obduracy, though entirely justified, brought down fury from liberal commentators. *Wygant* was forgotten, and so were all the qualifiers in *Sheet Metal Workers*.[48] We had lost. I privately offered to resign—an offer Attorney General Meese immediately declined.

On July 7, 1986, shortly after the *Sheet Metal Workers* decision, the Court agreed to take two affirmative-action cases for the next term, *United States* v. *Paradise* and *Johnson* v. *Santa Clara County*. Both cases had horrible facts, and we unsuccessfully explored ways to make these cases go away.

Paradise, which was part of Reynolds' post-*Stotts* campaign, involved our intervention in a consent decree directed at the Alabama state troopers. The decree was not only non-victim-specific but had a rigid preferential quota, rather than a flexible preference. Justices White, Powell, and O'Connor had all said in *Sheet Metal Workers* that they would not permit such quotas. Accordingly, I readily conceded that the preference did not have to be victim-specific.[49] I argued only that this one would not do. O'Connor and White stood with us, but Justice Powell joined the Brennan opinion approving the preference without comment,[50] even though I argued the case more or less according to the script Powell had written in *Sheet Metal Workers*. I guess the Alabama state troopers were just too much for him.

Johnson involved a voluntary affirmative-action plan

by a county government that had never been accused of discrimination. A male who was passed over for a job in favor of a marginally less qualified woman—the first woman ever employed in that job—sued under Title VII. This was not quite a repeat of *Weber*. It lacked the element of past discrimination, which lurked in the background of both *Weber* and *Griggs*. Once again Justice Brennan wrote, and more or less republished his *Weber* opinion. Justice O'Connor concurred because she thought the disparity raised enough of a hint of prior discrimination to make the plan permissibly remedial. Justice Scalia, who was new to the Court, wrote a dissent that was partially joined by Justice White. This was striking in itself, since White had been in the *Weber* majority. Both said they would overrule *Weber*. Justice Stevens said that, but for his respect for precedent, he would too.

Still Tickin'[51]

Had we not been encumbered by the treacherous tailwind from our perilous "victory" in *Stotts,* the defeat in *Johnson* might not have happened. We would have taken Powell's or White's line and urged an affirmance or at most some modification of the decree in *Sheet Metal Workers*. But that is the wisdom of hindsight—self-serving and unreliable. In the long run the defeats were healthy; they cleared the air of victim specificity, taking it off the table once and for all. And *Johnson* reaffirmed *Weber*. I was now free to formulate the administration's position on race.

With the loss of the Senate in the 1986 midterm election, legislative relief became unthinkable, so that the Supreme Court was the only available forum for our views. I had a seasoned nucleus of collaborators in my office, who shared some of my convictions and were exceptionally knowledgeable about the intricacies of the law: my Counselor, Don Ayer, and Glen Nager and Richard Taranto, two brilliant recent O'Connor clerks.

I concentrated on what I cared about: taming *Griggs,* with its pressure toward quotas, and establishing more firmly what Powell had said in *Wygant*—that the Constitution does not allow government-ordered preferences except for the most unusual and compelling reasons. As my last Court term approached, two cases loomed up that presented ideal vehicles.

In late 1987 the Court had requested the Solicitor General's view on whether it should take up a case in which Dade County, Florida, had established a 5-percent minority-business-enterprise set-aside (MBE).[52] MBEs are one of the worst kinds of preferences,[53] although they appealed to some parts of the President's constituency who were interested in black capitalism.[54] The preference is not remedial. It is pure social engineering—a kind of racial industrial policy. In fact, it had become a focus for corruption and evasion. A firm had no need to hire minority workers, so long as more than half the ownership was black.[55] It was a clear example of a "racial bloc grant," to use Justice Powell's phrase, and one likely to go to political entrepreneurs, not to the neediest or most deserving. But Congress loved MBEs, and the Supreme Court appeared to have approved them in a 1980 case, *Fullilove* v. *Klutznick*.[56] Although there had been no opinion for the Court, *Fullilove* had held by a 6–3 margin that such preferences did not necessarily violate the Constitution. Chief Justice Burger's plurality opinion was so narrow and qualified as to be virtually incomprehensible. *Fullilove* certainly did not establish that Congress had some special title to define the meaning of equal protection and its denial. Rather, it emphasized Congress's unique authority, under Section 5 of the Fourteenth Amendment, to determine if there had in fact been violations of equal protection, and then to remedy such violations. This last had been particularly important in the nineteenth century, when Congress's power over local matters was thought to be quite limited.

In the *Dade County* case, as in *Fullilove,* the local authority was acting under the umbrella of a federal grant program that required the MBE. There were those in the administration who wanted to "stand up and be counted" with a full-blown attack on *Fullilove* and MBEs. That was not, however, my feeling. The Court is reluctant to declare an Act of Congress unconstitutional. An attack on *Fullilove,* without first preparing the ground, would have been another kamikaze mission.

Fortunately, there was an alternative. We answered the Court's request by emphasizing the complexities of the particular case. We suggested that this would be a poor context in which to consider the status of MBEs. We pointed out that a much better case, *City of Richmond* v. *Croson,*[57] was making its way to the Court. *Croson* presented the issue in a crisp and uncomplicated way. An unusually high 30-percent MBE set-aside had been instituted not by the Congress of the United States but by the Richmond City Council, after a most perfunctory hearing at which no credible findings of past discrimination had been made. More-over, the court of appeals had struck down the set-aside as unconstitutional in the light of *Wygant*. Indeed, that court had adopted a stronger position than seemed right to me: the city could act only to remedy its own discrimination, and not that of private contractors and businesses within its jurisdiction. We proposed that the Supreme Court should hold the *Dade County* case in abeyance until it decided *Croson*, and then send *Dade County* back to the court of appeals for reconsideration. We then waited for *Croson*, where we would have our say. But two other critical cases had to be addressed before that time came.

Our opportunity to tame *Griggs* came in *Wards Cove Packing Co.* v. *Atonio*,[58] in which the Ninth Circuit Court of Appeals had bent even the most extreme interpretation of *Griggs* way out of shape in order to do what it saw as rough justice. The facts looked terrible, but when you looked more closely it was a perfect case in which to make our point.

Salmon canning in Alaska is a seasonal business, and each summer the packing companies hire workers for their factories as well as better-paid technicians, accountants, doctors, and office workers. The packers used a Seattle union hiring hall to supply their factory workers. The union membership was overwhelmingly Philippine, as was the work force the union supplied. At the remote summer factory sites the cannery workers were housed together and messed together on food preferred by Philippines. The noncannery workers were recruited from a variety of sources, and it seemed that the proportion of minority workers more or less reflected their availability in the various pools from which they were hired. Nonetheless, the court of appeals had held that, because of the extreme disparity between the percentage of minority cannery workers and those in the nicer noncannery jobs, the canneries had to justify their hiring practices for the noncannery positions. Thus, on the basis of this racial-stratification evidence, the canneries were forced either to validate their practices according to the *Griggs* business-necessity test, or to pay years of back wages to the Philippine plaintiffs.

Although the spectacle of a racially segmented work force (what Justice Stevens, in his dissenting opinion, later characterized as a "plantation economy") was unattractive, and the case presented other nasty details such as the designation of the machine that gutted the fish as "the iron chink," it was obvious that the Philippine workers were not the victims of discrimination. Indeed, the appearance of discrimination came about only because the canners employed "too many" Philippine cannery workers, not because they hired too few minority noncannery workers. The case seemed a perfect occasion to show how, once the redistributive, social-engineering mentality takes hold, mere considerations of law and logic are swamped.

But there was one more ghost to exorcise before we could get a clean approach to the problem of compelled racial preferences. This was the case of Brenda Lee Patterson, a black clerical worker in a small North Carolina credit union who for years had had to endure racially motivated harassment, insult, and lack of advancement. *Patterson* v. *McLean Credit Union*[59] was to be the case that stirred the greatest anxieties in the civil-rights community, and the harshest criticism of my conduct by what some call the conservative movement.

"More like a Dukakis Solicitor General"

Brenda Patterson sued her employer under Section
1981, a civil-rights statute enacted after the Civil War
as part of Reconstruction. It guaranteed, "all persons
. . . the same right in every State . . . to make and
enforce contracts . . . as is enjoyed by white citizens. . . ."[60] The Fourth Circuit Court of Appeals
had turned aside her suit on the ground that Section
1981—unlike Title VII of the Civil Rights Act of
1964—did not afford relief for harassment. The
extension of this early statute to private discrimination seemed a terrible stretch from its previous limited
application to Jim Crow legal disabilities imposed by
the former slave states. In the brief we filed the first
time around we described this distorted interpretation of the Act as "well-established."* The Civil Rights
Division and I agreed that, once that premise was
accepted, the decision to foreclose Patterson's

* This interpretation had a long and involved history. For about the
first century of their presence on the books, the Reconstruction-era
civil-rights statutes had consistently been interpreted according to the
obvious and natural meaning of their words: to strike down the legal
restrictions preventing the former slaves from acquiring and dealing in
property or making contracts. In the 1968 case of *Jones* v. *Alfred Mayer
Co.* the Supreme Court, over a devastating dissent by Justice Harlan,
held for the first time that a parallel Reconstruction-era provision
dealing with the right of former slaves to acquire property should be
interpreted to cover a private party's racially motivated refusal to sell a
house to a black. Thus the Supreme Court, in a *coup de main* extreme
even for the Warren Court, proclaimed to an astonished nation that the
fair-housing legislation that was painfully wending its way through
Congress had really sat undiscovered on the books for a hundred years.
In *Runyon* the Supreme Court, standing on the *Jones* precedent,
interpreted the parallel contracting provision to extend to a racially
motivated refusal by an all-white private academy in Arlington, Vir-
ginia, to accept an application from a black child.

claim would impose an artificial limit on a well-established doctrine. We showed that what had happened to Brenda Patterson was not just a generalized wrong but a violation of common-law contractual obligations of good-faith performance.

In the spring of 1988 the civil-rights community was shocked when, instead of deciding the *Patterson* case, the Court ordered reargument the next term on whether *Runyon* v. *McCrary*, the 1976 case that proclaimed the extension of Section 1981 to discrimination in private contracting, should be overruled. Considering that Robert Bork (so unjustly accused of racism) had supported the expansive interpretation of *Runyon* when he had been Solicitor General, it is ironic that this was one of Justice Kennedy's first acts after taking the seat to which Bork had originally been nominated. The order provoked not only a national outcry but a bitter dissent from Justices Brennan, Marshall, Blackmun, and Stevens. I was away from Washington when the reargument order came down, and Don Ayer reported that at the Attorney General's staff meeting that morning voices had been raised to the Attorney General saying that of course we would have to take our stand on this case, so as to "stiffen the spine" of "our people" on the Court. On my return, I went to see Meese and told him that, though I had not studied the matter, my initial inclination was that of TV comedian Ed Wynn, who kept an eleven-foot pole for things he wouldn't touch with a ten-foot pole. And the more I looked at the question, the more dangerous a trap it seemed.

To be sure, there was some sense behind the Court's willingness to reconsider the *Runyon* precedent. *Runyon* allowed a strange overlap between Title

VII and Section 1981. Section 1981 covered all contracts, including employment contracts covered by Title VII. Moreover, not only was *Runyon* a distortion of legislative language and history, but it had itself disregarded a century of "well-established" precedent.[61] Overruling *Runyon* would be a stinging symbolic and practical rebuke to the civil-rights community, and they were mobilizing a widespread effort at the reargument. On the other side, this seemed an equally dramatic occasion to show that an earlier era of strained and unprincipled adjudication was over.

The position of the United States would be crucial, and I was lobbied hard from all sides. I decided to regularize the process, inviting each side to make a formal presentation. To overrule a statutory precedent requires much more than an argument that the original decision was wrong. As Justice Scalia said to the employer's lawyer during the argument, "If that's all you have, I'm afraid it's nothing."

It was clear that I should not file a brief on reargument. There were no arguments other than the initial wrongness of *Runyon*. In Bork's time the United States had described the *Runyon* case as well established, and I myself had repeated that argument a few months ago, so any reversal would look like a last-gasp play by a departing administration. Most important of all, *Runyon* and Section 1981 dealt with old-fashioned bigotry. There were no *Griggs*-like effects tests here, no lurking pressures toward quotas or preference—just a prohibition on private discrimination. And, given the uproar, if the Court did overrule *Runyon*, Congress would restore the status quo in short order. Why, then, make a dramatic gesture that would confuse our goals, and jeopardize our upcoming efforts on the *Griggs* problem and in *Croson*—just for the sake of cleansing the books of an admittedly flawed precedent? On the other hand, a brief opposing overruling would be seen more as a gesture than as a substantive statement. We had already submitted a brief supporting Brenda Patterson. Our silence now would be an eloquent but respectful way of saying to the five members of the Court who had asked for reargument that this was a misconceived enterprise.

Unfortunately, some were not persuaded by these arguments and put intense pressure on Meese to overrule me and file a brief for overruling *Runyon*. At this time the Attorney General was in difficult personal straits. The Independent Counsel's investigation loomed large, and calls for his resignation were coming not only from his opponents but also from the Bush camp, which did not want to be embarrassed by him as the 1988 campaign got started. It was natural for Meese to turn to his hard-right supporters. In May and June of 1988 Meese and I discussed *Patterson* alone and at length. He made a clear decision not to overrule me, and I believe he did so because he thought it was right. It cannot have been easy for him. One of his supporters wrote him that if he did not fire me that would only show that he himself ought to resign. Paul Kamenar of the Washington Legal Foundation, referring to *Patterson* as well as my decision not to defend the constitutionality of a Texas statute outlawing flag desecration, told the press: "Fried seems to be running a renegade operation that looks more like a Dukakis solicitor general's office and if Meese doesn't fire him, it would substantiate what many people believe already—that Meese is the attorney general in name only."[62] And Pat McGuigan, of

Paul Weyrich's Free Congress Foundation, said: "If my friend Charles is uncomfortable with the legal philosophy of this administration, perhaps he should leave it and join the next one that comes along."[63]

With the resolution of the *Patterson* controversy, the way was clear for my office to write the briefs we wanted in *Croson* and *Atonio*. *Atonio* was intricate—largely Richard Taranto's work. We presented what no other party did, a carefully developed argument that went beyond the narrow, winning statistical point in the case. Building on the prior term's *Watson* brief written mainly by Glen Nager,[64] we suggested a fundamental clarification of the vaguely worded extravagances that Chief Justice Burger's *Griggs* opinion had opened up in the lower courts.

Croson was my particular project. Here too the crucial presentation would be the government's. First, I wanted to capture again the spirit of the *Wygant* brief. Next, it seemed important to appeal to Justice O'Connor. As the conscientious center of the Court, she tried to continue the traditions represented by Justice Powell, who had in turn looked back to Justice Harlan as his mentor. It seemed possible to persuade Justice O'Connor to accept now the line put forward by Justice Powell in *Wygant*. In this task Glen Nager's judgment and assistance were indispensable. Finally, it was important to break off from the extreme position taken by the court of appeals. Though we emphasized that the preferences in the Richmond plan would be permissible only as a remedy for specific and identifiable past discrimination, it seemed wrong to say that the city could act only to remedy its own past discrimination, and not that of others in its jurisdiction. No one else was pointing the Court in that middle direction. The city's lawyer defended the 30-percent set-aside as broadly remedial on a formula that differed in name only from societal discrimination, and the lawyer for the disappointed contractor took the Fourth Circuit's line. That seemed too rigid. It would mean, for instance, that a city could not pass an antidiscrimination ordinance applicable to anyone other than itself.[65] Once again we explicitly disclaimed victim specificity in a narrowly tailored, genuinely remedial plan. Of course, the Richmond plan met none of these conditions. It was a loose, ill-designed, unsupported, and crude political gesture.

Moghul paintings show magnificently caparisoned elephants striding into war. Perhaps a flea in the ear of such an animal imagines that it directs the vast beast's movements and wins the battle. Perhaps the 1988 term was so successful only because we had figured out where the Court—with Scalia and Kennedy replacing Burger and Powell—was going to go and had fit our submissions to that disposition.

Justice O'Connor's opinion in *Croson* was a firm and eloquent statement for the proposition that the Constitution protects all alike, and protects them as individuals, not as members of groups. Indeed, she went further, to state that the remedying of past discrimination was perhaps the only compelling governmental purpose to justify race-conscious preferences. And even then she made clear that such preferences, though they need not be victim-specific, must be strictly limited and could only be used when other, race-neutral measures had been shown to be ineffective.[66] Justice Scalia, in his separate opinion, went further, embracing both victim specificity and the Fourth Circuit's additional limitation on the remedial powers of the city.

In *Atonio,* Justice White's opinion disposed of the interpretations of *Griggs* that had pressured innocent employers to use quotas in order to avoid the expense and uncertainty of litigation. The outcry went up that *Atonio* had overruled *Griggs.* That is wrong. An employer who maintains requirements and practices that exclude minorities is still liable under Title VII. He must still put forward a plausible account of why such requirements are reasonably related to his business. The Court did insist, however, that the employer need justify only those practices that had been shown to have an exclusionary effect—it was not enough just to point to a statistical imbalance and then make the employer justify everything he did.

In *Patterson* the Court unanimously held that respect for precedent precluded overruling *Runyon* v. *McCrary.* But Justice Kennedy, writing for the majority, went on at length to reject the Solicitor General's argument that the old Civil Rights Act could extend beyond discrimination in initial hiring to cover racially motivated harassment on the job, denial of promotion, and discharge. It was odd to get a judicial scolding reminiscent of *Sheet Metal Workers* from that quarter.

Is the current disposition stable, and does it make sense? The point of tension is in the difference between *Croson,* which severely limits the use of preferences by government, and *Weber,* which seems to be much less restrictive of voluntary affirmative action in the private sector. There are those who would push *Weber* in the direction of *Croson,* finding it anomalous that two groups of employers often dealing with similar work forces doing similar jobs should operate under such different regimes. Justice Scalia, as I have said, would overrule *Weber* outright. As an original matter that would have brought us closer to the intention of the original Act. Still, I believe the Court in *Weber* had produced a sensible if jurisprudentially disingenuous result.

But the tension is in any event tolerable, and even appropriate. The yearning for symmetry and ideological purity has been the bane of this area of the law.[67] Elsewhere we accept the notion that governments are bound by stricter rules than are private actors. Private universities, for instance, are not and should not be bound by free-speech and Establishment Clause limits that apply to public institutions. The government, unlike private actors, is a monopolist whose regime we cannot escape, and therefore it makes sense to discipline the government far more tightly—particularly in an area like racial preferences, which can so easily degenerate into stifling political entrepreneurship and rent-seeking.

Discrimination is another matter and should be stamped out wherever it occurs. This, like all the most stringent injunctions of morality, is a negative—not a positive—duty. "Thou shalt not kill" is an injunction at once more absolute, more definite, and more readily enforced than "Love your neighbor as yourself." I am quite ready to see the government enforce the former, but not the latter.[68] Recall that without the Civil Rights Act private actors would be entirely free to practice the most odious discrimination, since the Constitution guarantees only equal protection of the laws—it operates only against government.

I do not think Justice Brennan was far off the mark when in *Weber* he celebrated "voluntary, private, race-conscious efforts to abolish traditional patterns of racial segregation and hierarchy." Of course, Justice Brennan has shown by his votes and opinions that the implicit qualifications and limitations in this statement were merely strategic, and that, given the opportunity, he would readily join those who would force a regime of preferences and quotas throughout the public and private sectors. And that is why Justice Scalia's push for clear rules mandating color-blindness everywhere has its attractions. It is a reflex related to the adoption of the doctrine of originalism, the attraction of a supposed cure for unprincipled, purely political judging. And yet that kind of definiteness is unattainable in any event, and its pursuit obscures the opportunity to establish humbler, more local truths. The public-private dichotomy is uneasy from both sides. It stinks in the nostrils of the leftist critics of our law.[69] It is the genius of the liberal state.

5

POWERS

*A judge . . . may be surprised at the
poverty of really useful and unambiguous
authority applicable to concrete problems
of executive power as they actually present
themselves. Just what our forefathers did
envision, or would have envisioned had
they foreseen modern conditions, must be
divined from materials almost as
enigmatic as the dreams Joseph was called
upon to interpret for Pharaoh.[1]*

*T*he competition between the President and the Congress is as old as the Republic. More is at stake than just political rivalry. In the end, it is about how ordinary citizens will experience the powers that order their lives—about how far those powers are responsible or even understandable to the people. The Reagan administration had a vision about the arrangement of government power: the authority and responsibility of the President should be clear and unitary. The Reagan years were distinguished by the fact that that vision was made the subject of legal, rather than simply political, dispute. The battle to rearrange government power was fought in the Supreme Court.[2] As Solicitor General, I was in the front line of this struggle—like my predecessor Rex Lee, who had won an important victory striking down the legislative veto.[3] I extended Lee's victory in *Bowsher* v. *Synar*, which struck down the provision of the Gramm-Rudman laws that put the Comptroller General's finger on the law's budget-cutting trigger. But in *Morrison* v. *Olson*, the Independent Counsel case, our efforts were soundly defeated, and the Sentencing Guidelines case put the last nail in their coffin.

The Independent Counsel Case

"That is what this suit is about. Power."[4] Justice Scalia spoke these words with deadly emphasis from the bench on the last day of term, June 29, 1988, in his lone dissent in *Morrison* v. *Olson*. The Independent Counsel law (Ethics in Government Act) had been enacted as a response to the "Saturday Night Massacre," when Richard Nixon fired Special Prosecutor Archibald Cox in an unsuccessful attempt to derail a criminal investigation into Watergate. The Act forces the Attorney General to ask a panel of judges to name an Independent Counsel, whose job it is to investigate and, if the evidence warrants it, indict and prosecute high administration officials. The Attorney General must ask for an Independent Counsel if outside information or his own preliminary inquiry turns up *any* reasonable grounds for further investigation.[5] The Act also puts the Attorney General under pressure to appoint an Independent Counsel if a matter is referred to him by certain members of Congress. Once appointed, the Independent Counsel proceeds to hire whatever staff he chooses, spend whatever resources he finds necessary, and take as long as he wishes in investigating the designated object.[6]

Justice Robert H. Jackson, when he was Attorney General in 1940, showed why such a scheme would be unfair and a danger to individual liberty. The "post of Federal District Attorney from the beginning has been safeguarded by presidential appointment" because,

> with the law books filled with a great assortment of crimes, a prosecutor stands a fair chance of finding at least a technical violation of some act on the part of almost anyone. In such a case, it is not a question of discovering the commission of a crime and then looking for the man who has committed it, it is a question of picking the man and then searching the law books, or putting investigators to work, to pin some offense on him. . . .[7]

And as Justice Scalia put it in his dissent in *Morrison:* "How frightening it must be to have your own independent counsel appointed with nothing else to do but investigate you."[8]

The *Morrison* litigation grew out of a fight between Olson, the head of the office, whose job it is to guard presidential prerogatives, and two Democratic congressional barons, Peter Rodino (of the Watergate Committee fame) and John Dingell. Their committees were dissatisfied with the EPA's enforcement of environmental laws, laws the Reagan administration considered examples of harmful overregulation. EPA Administrator Anne Burford claimed executive privilege,[9] on orders from the White House, as urged by Olson. Executive privilege is at once a showstopper and a red flag in a contest between Congress and the President. Burford's claim was like a declaration of war. Just how much the privilege protects executive officers in a congressional investigation has never been settled, and it is a fair bet that the Congress would just as soon keep it that way. What enraged Congress particularly was Olson's idea of asking a federal court to declare that the privilege was justified, thus seizing the initiative and heading off a contempt citation against Burford.[10] Congressional wrath descended on Olson, not just politically but personally. Chairman Rodino invoked the law in such a way that the Attorney General had no choice but to ask for an Independent Counsel to investigate Olson for criminally defying Congress. To those who knew Olson as an earnest young lawyer of the most rigorous probity, this was very unfair, and an example of the harm the Independent Counsel law could do.

The Independent Counsel law is at the heart of the debate about the separation of powers. Whenever the branches of government are in the hands of persons committed to strongly different philosophies, separation-of-powers issues loom large. This was true in the first Jackson administration; it was true of the early Roosevelt tenure vis-à-vis the Supreme Court; and it was true of the Reagan years. Reagan's program of deregulation had been frustrated by a large Democratic majority in the House.[11] That is why the administration's tactic had been to avoid pressing for legislative solutions, seeking instead deregulation by administrative inactivity. This was a weak and vulnerable tactic. Its indirectness made it seem devious and exposed a flaw at the place where legislation and administration meet: after all, the President is ordered by the Constitution to "take care that the laws be faithfully executed." Though discretion about enforcement belongs to the President, it goes too far to suggest that this allows him to disregard any law he disagrees with just because he disagrees with it.[12]

The need to discipline what the Constitution calls "officers" has two occasions. First, there has never been any doubt that in our system all officers are subject to the law like anyone else.[13] Second, officers are obligated to carry out the laws particular to their offices, and it is this second, political obligation that causes trouble.[14] But we have purposely confused the two concepts. Burford was threatened with criminal contempt; her assistant, Rita Lavelle, was sent to prison; and Olson was investigated for criminal offenses. But theirs were political offenses.[15] In Olson's case, what the House Committee did in forcing the appointment of an Independent Counsel fit exactly Robert Jackson's words: "It [was] a question of picking the man and then searching the law books . . . to pin some offense on him."

There is a dilemma here. If the legislative branch is too ready to punish its enemies, the executive may be too reluctant to investigate and prosecute its own. There are practical solutions. Special prosecutors can be named by the executive and given independent authority. Though this authority may be withdrawn, as it was in Nixon's firing of Archibald Cox, this can only be done at ruinous political cost to the President. But after Watergate this was not enough to satisfy Congress, which was bent on asserting itself and disciplining the executive. The Independent Counsel law was the result.

Many conservatives thought the Independent Counsel law was an outrage, but the politics were such that we were scared to challenge it. The challenges would have come most naturally in Iran-Contra and in respect to Attorney General Meese's own involvement with the Wedtech scandal. But these were terrible cases in which to challenge a law that the public was told guaranteed impartial justice. Accordingly, one of the most imaginative of the administration's legal officials, Richard Willard, proposed a solution that would both satisfy the public and save some shadow of the President's rights: to offer the Independent Counsels chosen by the court in accordance with the Act parallel appointments in the Department of Justice under departmental regulations guaranteeing them appropriate independence and discretion. Thus a challenge would not reach the courts, since every action such a prosecutor took—the indictments he signed, the subpoenas he issued—would be doubly valid, based in the Independent Counsel law and the President's inherent powers, and so no one could raise the separation-of-powers claim to question the prosecutor's authority. Lawrence Walsh and James McKay, the best and most conscientious of the court-appointed Independent Counsels, were most interested in getting about their work, and so accepted the arrangement. As a result, the Iran-Contra and Meese investigations were immunized from constitutional challenge. Alexia Morrison, the Independent Counsel in the EPA-Olson matter, would not accept the parallel appointment, and the stage was set for an inevitable challenge. Though the context of this case was far better, there was still the political implication that we were just looking for a way to protect the President and his cronies. I dreaded the response of the courts in this atmosphere. But Ted Olson was the defendant, and there was no way for me to keep the case out of the courts.

The challenge to the law came up in 1987 in a side issue. By early 1988 a powerful decision in the court of appeals striking down the law on all the challenged grounds—violation of the Appointments Clause of the Constitution, invasion of a core executive function, improper assignment of administrative functions to the judiciary—gave us in the Justice Department heart.[16] The Supreme Court was to hear the case by April. Since newly appointed Justice Kennedy had recused himself, an equally divided Supreme Court would affirm the court of appeals. Both Rehnquist and Scalia had served as head of the Office of Legal Counsel; surely strict separation-of-powers logic must be in their blood. The Court's most ardent liberal, William Brennan, had written some very strong separation-of-powers opinions,[17] and he might also be responsive to the potential for oppression of individuals in this law.

The Supreme Court chamber—a marble cube in a

style I would describe as neo-Caligula—had never been as full as for that argument. Many Senators were there. Ted Olson found a seat by getting in line at five in the morning. I was too caught up in the heat of battle to read the portents in the courtroom that morning. Alexia Morrison argued first. She sensibly stuck to describing the mechanics of the law, and the Justices' questions gave the impression that they were trying to make sure they had the details of the law right. The inquiry emphasized the law's safeguards and the limits on the Independent Counsel's discretion. In practice—as Morrison's own behavior, and that of some of the other Independent Counsels showed—these limits were formal and ineffective. Olson's lawyer, Tom Martin, tried to point this out. He too was questioned about the details of the law, though, I remember thinking, rather more sharply and more skeptically than Morrison.

It was up to me to make the structural, constitutional argument. I made two points. First, the Act violated the Appointments Clause of the Constitution by vesting the appointment of the Independent Counsel not in the President or the head of an executive department but in another branch of government: the judiciary. The Constitution says that officers of the United States shall be appointed by the President, with Senate confirmation.[18] The clause goes on to state that "inferior officers" can be appointed by the President, the courts, or department heads, however Congress provides. My point was that the Independent Counsel was hardly an inferior officer. Also, it made little sense to read the clause to allow cross-branch appointments of inferior officers: courts should not appoint Assistant Secretaries of

State, any more than the Attorney General should appoint clerks of court. Admitting the difficulty of making the distinction between principal and inferior officers, forbidding cross-branch appointments seemed a particularly sensible way to read the clause, since very little would be made to turn on that difficult distinction.

My second point was to confront the concern that only through an independent counsel can executive officers be subject to the law. Referring to the Watergate episode (which, like sex in the Victorian era, was on everyone's mind though no one would speak of it), I made the argument that a special prosecutor— formally within the executive establishment, like any other prosecutor—had sufficient political safeguards to protect his independence. After all, Nixon's firing of Archibald Cox, regrettable and improper though it had been, was not a defeat for the rule of law. In fact, the rule of law prevailed in spite of the Saturday Night Massacre. For the first time in our history, I pointed out, a President had been driven from office.

Justice Stevens posed a number of counterexamples to my Appointments Clause argument—court appointments of interim United States Attorneys, grand juries, and the Reconstruction-era practice of court-appointed election commissioners in the Southern states.[19] But among the lawyers that morning I alone was allowed to make my argument with little interruption. The absence of dialogue is often ominous, and it should have suggested to me that the Justices had made up their minds and were not going to tip their hands by engaging the Solicitor General in discourse. I think of the contrast to my abortion argument a year later, when the Court was divided.

Then the questioning was probing, continuous, and engaging. Two months after it was argued, the decision in *Morrison* came down. Only Justice Scalia voted against the law.[20]

Three Ways of Looking at Separation of Powers

Scalia set out the geometric view: our government is divided into three distinct branches, independent except in the specific ways the Constitution itself provides for interaction.[21]

He began reading his dissent by quoting from the Massachusetts Constitution of 1780:

> In the government of this commonwealth, the legislative department shall never exercise the executive and judicial powers, or either of them; the executive shall never exercise the legislative and judicial powers, or either of them; the judicial shall never exercise the legislative and executive powers, or either of them; to the end it may be a government of laws, and not of men.

This prologue assumes a distinct meaning for each of the individual terms. Of course, unlike the Massachusetts Constitution (and unlike the Declaration of the Rights of Man promulgated by the revolutionary French National Assembly in 1789), the federal Constitution does not mention the separation of powers.[22] If we are going to derive anything like Scalia's strict separation principle from the Constitution, it will have to be by a process of inference. Even the Constitution's intellectual ancestors—Locke, Blackstone, Montesquieu—were concerned more with achieving what was called a balanced constitution and did not embrace any such rigorous principle. As in Madison's essay concerning "ambition checking ambition" in *The Federalist Papers,* No. 51, these men sought to exploit whatever competing and distinct interests they found at hand to assure that government would not be overly prompt and effective in responding to the direction of any particular interest. They liked the idea of a government that would be more likely to leave men alone. Certainly they had at best a guarded and ambivalent interest in assuring that kind of strong, coherent, and efficacious leadership (Hamilton praised it as "muscular") that can best be offered by a preeminent and unitary executive.

Scalia's central point about the Independent Counsel law was that prosecution of crime is an executive function. Here the often murky and conflicting theories of the main separation-of-powers advocates agree: the application of general rules to particular individuals is at the heart of the executive function; just as the executive must not be allowed to make up the rules and enforce them, so the legislature must not be allowed to apply the laws to individuals after having made them up. But in the Independent Counsel law, the Congress did not appear to intrude on the "core" executive function in this way at all. There the invasion of the executive function was in giving the appointment of the prosecutor to a court and then leaving her largely unsupervised.[23]

It may not be readily apparent why this is a violation of the separation of powers. Although she was appointed by a court to an executive office, why was the Independent Counsel not thereafter just another executive officer, exercising an executive function? The answer lies in what separation-of-powers geometricians—and Hamilton before them in *The Federalist Papers*[24]—designate as the concept of the unitary executive: It is not enough that each department "shall never exercise the . . . powers" of either of the other two. The functions of each department should be exercised only by the single institution—courts, Congress, the President—designated as having that power. The power may not be split among several legislatures, several executives. Thus, as I argued to the Court in *Morrison,* the first section of each of the first three Articles of the Constitution assigns *"all* legislative power herein granted" to the Congress; *"the* executive power"[25] to the President; *"the* judicial power of the United States" to the Supreme Court and whatever inferior federal courts Congress establishes. Any movement beyond these three establishments threatens the prescribed tripartite architecture. Thus executive functions must be exercised only by the President or by officials securely responsible to him.[26] This last point—that not only must executive power be kept separate from the other two branches, but also the President's establishment must be firmly unified under his control—was the heart of Scalia's dissent. It was also the point that most threatened established power centers in Congress and the bureaucracy.

It is as important that the executive be unitary as that its functions not be usurped by Congress. The establishment of many centers of executive power could lead to a babble of incoherent, conflicting executive authorities. As the authority of the President is diminished, that of the Congress grows and threatens to become the very legislative tyranny that the framers explicitly sought to avoid and counterbalance. In the end, the President would be reduced to a ceremonial head of state.

Scalia's is the best statement of the rigorous view of separation of powers. The view that defeated it was announced by William Rehnquist, the new Chief Justice.[27] It is not particularly deep or satisfying. Rehnquist's opinion asked two questions. First, does the scheme of the Independent Counsel law literally violate any specific constitutional provision? Concluding that the Independent Counsel was an inferior officer and that neither the constitutional language nor constitutional practice forbids cross-branch appointments, the Chief brushed aside my Appointments Clause objections. Second, as to separation of powers more generally, the Court concluded that the authority of the President was not trammeled "too much," and that in any event Congress was not "aggrandizing" itself at the President's expense.

The deeper competition to Scalia's conception of the separation of powers had been stated by Justice White in a series of dissents in earlier cases in which the Court had seemed to be moving in Scalia's direction.[28] Justice White sees Congress as charged not just with the task of making substantive rules of policy, but with setting up the government: establishing departments and offices, defining their powers and responsibilities. All questions of the organization of the government and of the relations between the parts are left open, to be resolved as a matter of legislative judgment as the Congress thinks "necessary and proper." In practice this view may reach the same conclusions as the Chief Justice's in *Morrison,* but it is at once more profound and more systematic. For it does not meet constitutional objections with a shrug—where is it written that this may not be done? Rather, it proposes a general theory of government, a theory of legislative supremacy. It has a distinct affinity with the British notion of parliamentary sovereignty and recalls the progressive era's flirtation with the parliamentary system as a more up-to-date conception of government.

If we are concerned with finding pragmatic ways for power to check power—"ambition checking ambition," as Madison put it—then it does not matter too much how we designate the competing powers. In the Roman Republic, the supreme magistracy was held by two Consuls, each of whom could veto any act of the other. The division of the Legislative Branch into two Houses is another example of such a contingent arrangement.[29] The history of bicameralism in our constitutional story[30] does not support the rigorous geometric view of the separation of powers but, rather, illustrates another, quite different, and probably dominant strand in the origin of the doctrine of the separation of powers: the separation not of functions but of social *orders*—King, Lords, Commons.[31] As constitutional reflection turned more toward organization than class, the example of monarchy provided both a bridge and a source of confusion. The monarch was often thought of as an embodiment of the sovereign authority of the nation as a whole[32] and also as more likely to be an efficient manager than large, deliberative assemblies.

Theoretical Antecedents

The principal classical theorists of separation of powers were concerned almost exclusively with the executive and legislative functions.[33] Rousseau and Locke asked if there was a distinction between execution and legislation, and both gave sharply affirmative answers. But their reasoning was very different, and their followers certainly drew very different practical conclusions.

For Rousseau, the separation of powers was a direct corollary to his main thesis: that all legitimate authority comes from and remains in the people alone. The general will of the people is the only proper source of law, and as such it is indivisible and inalienable.[34] Only the people as a whole, the general will, can be legislative, and that function cannot be delegated to a smaller body. But *government* can and indeed must be carried out through agents of the people. Hence the very notion of "the government" is a Rousseauean invention. It is these two powers, nation and government, that must be kept distinct.[35]

It is striking to see what life has made of this. It was doomed from the start in France and every other major state of Enlightenment Europe. That is why the Abbé Sieyès, the great theorist of the revolutionary constitutional debates, insisted that the Assembly *was* the nation.[36] This was the reigning analysis throughout the revolutionary years. Since the Assembly represented the sovereign nation, what, then, of government? Ministers were reduced to the status of functionaries (the word "bureaucrat" was coined at that time precisely to describe their status), who implemented the policies of the Assembly under the strict supervision of committees of representatives. (The Committees of Public Safety and of General Security were the best known of these overseers.) As one representative at the time put it, the executive is whatever is left over when legislation ends.

Locke's theory of the separation of powers had a far more congenial center of gravity. Locke accepted the concept of representation as inevitable. Because both the executive and the legislative powers drew their authority from the people, neither need be radically subordinated to the other.[37] And in describing their coordinate authority, Locke recurred not to the logic of sub-ordination but, rather, adopted as his intermediate premise the concept we today recognize as the rule of law. The citizens' rights and duties vis-à-vis one another and particularly vis-à-vis the state must be defined in general terms in order to assure impartiality and the kind of stability, definiteness,[38] and therefore predictability and security that come from general rules. And the executive is the agency that is responsible for enforcing these rules and thereby procuring peace and security according to them.

But Locke recognized a managerial function of the executive when he wrote of the "prerogative" power: "Many things there are which the law can by no means provide for; and those must necessarily be left to the discretion of him that has the executive power in his hands."[39] The executive has the management not only of foreign affairs but also of the common wealth of the nation, a concept that was assumed to be limited by the very fact that private rights and private wealth made up the largest part of what was significant in the ordinary life of ordinary citizens.

Executive Power: Prerogative in the Administrative State

The framers looked to Locke. What Locke called the prerogative powers have to do with the management of the nation's resources (the royal patrimony in Locke's day). In the modern administrative-welfare state, however, the prerogative powers assigned to the executive cover all the resources, prerogatives, and discretion enjoyed within the national establishment. And the President (or Prime Minister) is expected to have a policy about almost everything, since so many laws, institutions, and structures leave considerable scope for discretion in their administration.

The issue of separation of powers might be rephrased to ask, By what authority does the executive have a policy at all? One answer—and it was exploited fully by Jefferson, Wilson, and Franklin Roosevelt—is that he has a project for the nation as the head of his political party. This is not the answer that the Reagan administration gave. President Reagan was a master at using his position to speak directly to the nation, but he tried equally to accomplish his plans by using what he said were the prerogatives of his office—not by his authority as chief of his political party. Iran-Contra grew out of an assertion of presidential powers; similarly, President Nixon sought to make use of these "prerogative" powers in the impoundment controversy[40] and in his attempted use of the IRS to punish his political enemies.

In Locke's rule-of-law view of the separation of powers, policy would seem to be a matter of general rules, determined by the legislature. But the legal space Locke opened up with the prerogative powers, and the moral space opened up by the natural prestige of the executive, widen when Congress is able to legislate only the barest outlines of programs covering large parts of the nation's life. If the Congress must leave so much discretion, delegating all of this power to institutions substantially independent of the President, then the executive is severely weakened; it is kept from its basic job of applying general rules to particular circumstances.

This dilemma was illustrated more than 150 years ago in the controversy over the Second Bank of the United States. Chartered by an Act of Congress in 1816, by 1829 the bank had become perhaps the most powerful institution in the nation. It had branches throughout the country, could issue notes which circulated like currency, and had an assured and enormous base derived from the Treasury's use of the bank as the depository of United States funds. Andrew Jackson shared a popular resentment of so powerful an institution that had public responsibilities but was subject to no public accountability. He determined to destroy the bank. Its partisans in Congress had overplayed their hand and got through a bill to renew the bank's charter some four years before its expiration. Jackson vetoed the bill. Though the bank still had a long lease on life, Jackson was determined to kill it. His most effective blow was the withdrawal of the funds of the United States from the bank. No law required the bank to be the sole and official depository for government funds, but it was assumed that it would be when the bank was set up.[41] By what authority, then, could Jackson pursue a policy at odds with the legislation chartering the bank? As far as Jackson was concerned, his warrants were his electoral mandate and the actual management which he as head of the executive had over the assets of the government—the prerogative power.[42]

There was an important hitch. The authority over the deposits of the United States lay not with the President, but with the Secretary of the Treasury. Indeed, very few of the powers of the executive belong to the President as such; rather, they reside in designated heads of departments and other subordinate officers. Jackson urged his Secretary of the Treasury, William J. Duane, to withdraw the funds. Duane silently but stubbornly refused. Finally, he was dismissed and replaced by Jackson's close adviser, the Attorney General and future Chief Justice, Roger B. Taney, who did the deed. And in 1836 the Treasury issued the Species Circular, directing that the notes of the bank would no longer be accepted in payment of obligations to the United States.

This episode, repeated in various forms many times throughout our history,[43] makes three related points about the separation of powers. First, it illustrates how, the more government does, the larger the discretion identified by Locke becomes. Second, it shows that Congress cannot set out all the details about how this discretionary space should be filled up. And, third, controlling the subordinate officers in charge of this discretionary space is often the political battlefield for control over policy. That is why questions about the appointment power and the removal power loom so large. This is why I argued to the Court (successfully) in the Gramm-Rudman case that the Comptroller General is an officer of the Congress, since he is removable not by the President but only by joint resolution of Congress. It is why I argued (unsuccessfully) that the Independent Counsel law was unconstitutional because the Independent Counsel does not serve at the pleasure of the President. And it is why the Reagan administration, following the lead of President Carter, instituted by Executive Order a procedure requiring all agencies in the presidential establishment to submit their proposed regulations for review in the Executive Office of the President, specifically in the Office of Management and Budget.[44]

Executive Power and the Rule of Law

The President may be constrained by law, as may his officers; where the law is clear enough, it will be enforced by courts. That is one of the teachings of *Marbury* v. *Madison,* made explicit in 1838 in *Kendall* v. *United States.*[45] The President has the veto to fend off laws that hem him in too much, and he has whatever prestige he finds in and brings to his office. Beyond that, he is indeed the creature of the law. Difficulties arise because of the immense discretion that has developed as the reach of government in general has expanded in the welfare-administrative state. The problem has been how to get the advantages of effective, flexibile administration without compromising the two other, overriding values that the separation of powers is intended to serve: the protection of individual *liberty;* and the assurance of *accountability* to the people, who are the source of all law and authority—though individual rights must not be seen as depending on popular will.

Assuring the liberty of the subject against the arbitrary impositions of government may seem to be a very different concern from maintaining the separation of powers against Congress's efforts to contain the prerogative power in the modern administrative state. The citizen who is imposed upon may feel just as hurt whether he is the victim of an executive act or one mandated by Congress.[46] Indeed, the executive itself, in order to operate in a coherent and manageable way, must establish rules and procedures for its internal operations, and often the executive will be held to its own rules about how it will deal with others.

But individual liberty, accountability, and the rule of law mean more than just making sure that the ways in which the executive's authority is brought to bear on individuals are bureaucratically regular. We can get bureaucratic regularity without separation of powers and a unitary executive; if that were enough, we could just follow Justice White down the path of parliamentary sovereignty. But the separation of powers is more than a practical instrument, as the majority of the Court seem to believe. It is an expression of the deep structure of governmental power over human affairs.

If we are to keep our liberty in a world where powers of every sort are set above us, we must be able not only to predict and escape the imposition of power, but also to comprehend and control it. The political-science jargon speaks of "accountability." Accountability is only part of what is at stake. For although subjecting the executive to the control of elected representatives seems to increase accountability, this is an accountability that splits loyalty and may even saddle the chief executive with servants and advisers in whom he has lost confidence—perhaps even with spies and enemies. So it is not so much the accountability of power as its transparency that is at stake. The lines of responsibility should be stark and clear, so that the exercise of power can be comprehensible, transparent to the gaze of the citizen subject to it.

The separation of powers is important because it lets the ordinary citizen know who it is that exercises power over him. When the legislature makes laws, it acts in an entirely public way. And when a court exercises its particular power, it also publishes a text—a judgment or sentence. It is in the execution of the law that Kafka's castle looms. It is for administration that that peculiarly modern term "bureaucracy" is coined. It is there that power seems to be wielded by everyone and no one. This is the management of the prerogative domain, the use—or misuse—of the prerogative powers. No amount of rules and regularity can do enough to make these exercises of power transparent to their subjects.

In the end, what is needed is a clear focus of responsibility. Locke and Hamilton saw this focus in the person of the chief executive. As democratic as Locke was, he evidently relished the strong presence of the executive. As Hamilton said:

> A feeble executive implies a feeble execution of the government. A feeble execution is but another phrase for bad execution; and a government ill executed, whatever it may be in theory, must be, in practice, a bad government.[47]

Celebrations of executive power are not simply yearnings for efficiency. Locke and Hamilton craved clarity. They saw in a muddle about power the threat of chaos, and so a threat to liberty. That is why it seems natural to pin the responsibility for management on one person. It is also why even the revolutionaries of France were for a time loath to do without the King. In a unified executive we look through the legalisms of power to a person. Since we know whom to hold responsible, that person can take responsibility, and there is a greater chance for liberty. Where the focus of responsibility is diffused and blurred—the firing squad as the ultimate manifestation of bureaucracy—the threat to liberty is great.

Nowhere is this threat more clearly realized than in the definitions of the relation between the executive and his subordinates. From the beginning of our nation, sentiments of rivalry and resentment and a desire to wield power without responsibility have moved Congress to try to loose the ties that bind the President to his establishment. As we have seen in the case of President Jackson and Secretary Duane, the power of command must entail the power to enforce the command by removal. Anything else is equivocation. And if the President cannot command his own servants, then power is focused everywhere and nowhere.

The Headless Fourth Branch

To the revolutionaries in the Reagan administration, the independence of the independent regulatory commissions (for instance, the ICC, FTC, FCC, SEC, and, most imposingly, Federal Reserve Board) was an offense against the principles of the unitary executive and of the separation of powers. These agencies' independence of presidential authority was considered the extreme example, a kind of emblem, of one of the biggest obstacles to the administration's program. This obstacle was the informal network of experienced bureaucrats, congressional staffers, lobbyists who had once belonged to one of the other two categories, and partisan journalists. They made up "the permanent government" of the United States. They could be counted upon to raise a cry if mere political appointees came close to touching their favored programs. Protected by civil-service tenure, immensely knowledgeable about the details of the programs they administer, and skillful in the ways of bureaucratic manipulation, the permanent government could run circles around most presidential political appointees. These latter often did not know the details of the programs of which they were nominally in charge, and in any event they had to rely on the permanent government to implement their directives.

In a sense, the persistence of this situation was the President's own fault; after all, he had the authority to choose Cabinet and sub-Cabinet officers who would insist on managing their agencies in accordance with the President's program.[48] David Stockman, for example, was the model of the presidential appointee; by intelligence, knowledge, and hard work he was able to master the details of his task and thereby impose his will. There is, however, a limited supply of people like David Stockman.

The independence of the independent agencies is primarily due to the fact that their members do not—like most officers in the Executive Branch—serve at the pleasure of the President. Rather, under a variety of statutory formulations, they may be removed only for misbehavior.[49] President Roosevelt wrote FTC Commissioner William E. Humphrey, a Hoover appointee, in 1933: "You will, I know, realize that I do not feel that your mind and my mind go along together on either the policies or the administering of the Federal Trade Commission, and, frankly, I think it is best for the people of this country that I should have a full confidence. . . ." The Supreme Court held that this was not a sufficient basis for Humphrey's removal.[50]

The arguments advanced to justify these agencies have varied over time. At first there was a great deal of talk about the technical, almost scientific nature of their determinations. But since these agencies obviously make policy choices, and since other questions at least as scientific or as objective are regularly assigned to agencies squarely within the President's establishment,[51] this argument will not hold water. Also, the Administrative Procedure Act now enjoins such a degree of regularity and provides so much judicial review of Executive Branch decisions that concerns about due process and legality offer no reason to insist on independence.[52]

What remains is the heart of the matter. Congress has turned to the device of the independent agency in order to regulate a subject, while keeping policy-making power out of the President's hands. Congress did not just want the independent agencies to be independent of the President. Congress hoped and suspected that these agencies would in fact be quite dependent—on Congress. So there is plenty of political influence. (The savings and loan banks were regulated by such an "independent agency," which was notoriously responsive to congressional pressure.) What is lacking is accountability and transparency. This is why the Reagan revolutionaries targeted the independent agencies. It was hoped that a decision in the Supreme Court would hold that agency commissioners served at the pleasure of the President, and that statutory limitations on their removal were unconstitutional.

Consider these words:

> These independent commissions ... are in reality miniature independent governments. ... They constitute a headless "fourth branch" of the Government, a haphazard deposit of irresponsible agencies and uncoordinated powers. They do violence to the basic theory of the American Constitution that there should be three major branches of the Government and only three. ...
>
> . . .
>
> But though the commissions enjoy power without responsibility, they also leave the President with responsibility without power. Placed by the Constitution at the head of a unified and centralized Executive Branch, and charged with the duty to see that the laws are faithfully executed, he must detour around powerful administrative agencies which are in no way subject to his authority and which are, therefore, both actual and potential obstructions to his effective over-all management of national administration. ... The President is held responsible for the wise and efficient management of the Executive Branch of the Government. The people look to him for leadership. And yet we whittle away the effective control essential to that leadership by parceling out to a dozen or more irresponsible agencies important powers of policy and administration.

This was written not by any architect of the Reagan administration's separation-of-powers strategy, but for President Franklin Roosevelt in the 1937 Brown-law Report.[53]*

I did not come to my office committed to this program of submitting the independent agencies to the President's power, but here more than anywhere else the Attorney General's attraction to theoretical discussion had its effect. There were a number of workshops on the subject of the separation of powers in the Department. On January 9, 1987, the Attorney General chaired a seminar on the subject and invited outside academic participation. I was convinced. I had to be, since in the end this battle would have to be waged by me in the Supreme Court.

But it seemed to me that this was not a result that could be achieved by one bold stroke. By 1987 we had made considerable progress toward gaining acceptance for a rigorous conception of the separation of powers by virtue of the Supreme Court's decisions in the *Chadha* and *Bowsher* (Gramm-Rudman) cases. Yet there was great skittishness on the subject too. Fresh in people's minds was the history of how Paul Volker, the very independent-minded Federal Reserve Board Chairman, had almost single-handedly broken the inflation of the previous decade. And the established powers in and out of Congress, who knew how to manipulate the independent agencies for their own ends, could be counted on to resist any changes in

---

* Roosevelt's letter of transmittal adds: "The plain fact is that the present organization and equipment of the executive branch of the Government defeats the constitutional intent that there be a single responsible Chief Executive to coordinate and manage the departments and activities in accordance with the laws enacted by the Congress. Under these conditions the Government cannot be thoroughly effective in working, under popular control, for the common good."[54]

them. It seemed to me that this was a campaign that would have to proceed step by step, rather like the NAACP's brilliant campaign against state-imposed segregation.[55] They would not have prevailed had they brought the *Brown* v. *Board* suit prematurely.

Now, this strategy is not as sneaky as it sounds. The Court knows what is at stake, but it wants to go a step at a time. So, if you announce that a particular short step you want to take in a particular case is really part of a grand design, then the Court will feel as if you are trying to commit *it* to more than the case at hand requires. It is important not to crowd the Court, since your agenda may not yet be their agenda. This is particularly true of the Solicitor General. Unlike that of most litigants, his vision is supposed to extend beyond each particular case. I had my nose rubbed in this during my argument of the Gramm-Rudman case.

Immediately before my turn to speak, Michael Davidson, the counsel for the Senate, had concluded his defense of the law by saying that our attack entailed "throwing overboard" the Federal Reserve Board, the SEC, and in fact all the independent regulatory agencies. Actually, I had combed out of our brief any direct attack on the independent agencies. We objected first that the Comptroller General was a congressional agent and so could not engage in execution of the law. Only second did we make the point that, if he were an executive officer, then his functions under the law were so pervasive and so much at the core of the execution of all the laws that, like the Secretaries of State and Defense, he at least must serve at the pleasure of the President. So, having been that careful, when I got up to argue I felt justified in saying that Davidson's contentions were just "scare tactics." To this came a response from Justice O'Connor that was picked up in all the newspapers: "Well, Mr. Fried, you certainly scared me." I doubt any of the Justices were scared, but it was clear that few were ready to enlist in our project.

The fact of the matter is that the project had already broken cover—as Justice O'Connor's remark showed. Ted Olson, the head of the Office of Legal Counsel in the first Reagan term, was now in private practice and looking around for a case in which to make the attack on the independent agencies as a private litigant. And all of us in the Department were sent scrambling for ways to make his cases go away. What really put the cat among the pigeons was one of the Attorney General's famous speeches, this one to the Federal Bar Association, in which he frankly and bluntly questioned the status of the independent agencies. Though everyone knew we probably agreed with Ted Olson, what the Attorney General says gives an inescapable aura to all of our particular and carefully circumspect Court submissions. Richard Willard and I did everything we could to avoid having the next step in the project come up as a test of the constitutionality of the Independent Counsel law. That law had too strong an appeal to the public's common sense. The targets were too vulnerable (including Attorney General Meese himself). And the spectacle of the administration launching this rather arcane argument of principle in order to ward off investigations of the President's close friends was just too unattractive. As I feared and should have predicted, not only the particular attack but the whole enterprise ran aground and was smashed to pieces.

Epitaph: The Sentencing Guidelines

The Sentencing-Guidelines case, *Mistretta* v. *United States*,[56] was the last episode in our separation-of-powers project. In fact, the decision came down on January 18, 1989—two days before the end of the President's term, and on the morning of the farewell party for me at the Supreme Court. The guidelines represented a tough policy on crime, but they also played fast and loose with separation-of-powers principles.

The sentencing guidelines had been devised under the Sentencing Reform Act of 1984. The Act had been a bipartisan effort in the Congress, strongly supported by the Department of Justice, and capping years of effort to do something about the scandal of disparities in federal criminal sentencing. In an earlier day indefinite sentences had been the great progressive reform of the professional penologists. Expert parole boards would make individualized decisions after a person had served some time and the professionals had been able to make their evaluation of his response to rehabilitative efforts. Few liberal shibboleths had come into such general disrepute as this one.[57] No one had any confidence in the penal system's ability to identify repeat offenders or to reform: it punished, it deterred, and it took dangerous people out of circulation. What the system did allow were enormous, inexplicable, and grossly unfair disparities in sentences. Sentences would vary by many years, depending on the district, or the judge, or the race or sex or social status of the offender, or on nothing at all other than the length of the sentence that same judge may have given out in the case just before.[58]

Most agreed that it would be best to have fixed and uniform sentences, imposed at conviction, with no parole. The only problem was setting such sentences for the hundreds of offenses in the federal criminal code. Congress was not up to the job, which clearly required a good bit of trial-and-error. Also, even if the job could have been done once and for all, each decision was so fraught with policy and political and rhetorical and philosophical aspects that the task as a whole would overwhelm Congress. The device that Congress and the Department of Justice hit upon was to appoint a seven-person commission, consisting of at least three federal judges and the rest correctional professionals. A representative of the Attorney General would sit with the Commission as a nonvoting member. This United States Sentencing Commission, whose members would be named by the President and confirmed by the Senate, would develop sentencing guidelines according to general criteria set out in the Sentencing Reform Act, and lay them before the Congress. If Congress did not disapprove or modify them, they would become law. And this Commission would monitor their own handiwork and propose changes, which would also periodically be laid before Congress and also take effect if not disapproved. The Act passed Congress overwhelmingly and was signed into law in 1984 by President Reagan. Every faction would get some of what it wanted. Penal reformers would get the predictable and uniform sentences justice required. The law-and-order faction would get stiffer sentences for violent criminals, career criminals, and drug offenders. And the punishment for major white-collar criminals would for the first time match that imposed on criminals from less favored backgrounds. For the first time large-scale tax evaders, stock manipulators, and antitrust violators would serve significant prison terms.

During the Meese attorney-generalship the Commission became embroiled in a number of the Department's political and philosophical preoccupations. The death penalty had always been an emblem of the Meese Justice Department. It was thought to symbolize the difference between the belief in individual responsibility, and the left-liberal unwillingness to blame the offender. In the mid-seventies, when the Supreme Court laid down strict new rules for death sentences, it effectively abolished the federal death penalty until a careful revision by Congress could revive it. But some in Congress were determined at whatever cost to prevent such a revival of the death penalty—foremost among them Senator Kennedy, who had been one of the prime architects of the Sentencing Reform Act.

In 1986 and 1987 a scheme was hatched to bring about a general revival of the federal death penalty through the sentencing guidelines.[59] The guidelines could provide for the consideration of the mitigating and aggravating circumstances which the Supreme Court insisted on. This would then be laid before the Congress as part of an enormous package. Liberal opponents of the death penalty would then face (in an election year) a stark and unpopular dilemma. The argument by which the Commission's enabling legislation would permit consideration of the death penalty was clever, intricate, and not wholly specious. It was also entirely clear that the enabling legislation would never have passed had such a use been thought possible. Though I have no objections—moral or constitutional—to the death penalty, I felt strongly that, if there was to be a general federal death penalty,[60] it would have to come as a result of a full and frank confrontation in the Congress. The Supreme Court would never allow a person to be executed on the basis of the complicated logic the Department was urging on the Sentencing Commission. I expressed this view. I had to, because I did not want to have to do so for the first time when I was asked to raise the issue in the Supreme Court.

But it never came to that. The Commission voted to defer indefinitely any consideration of the death-penalty issue. And this then raised the other philosophical issues implicit in the scheme: separation of powers and presidential prerogative. Since the commissioners were appointed by the President, they should be subject to his orders. And if the commissioners refused to obey, they should be removable—even though the Act specifically provided for fixed terms and removal only for cause. Here was a test of the proposition raised in the case of the independent agencies, and it intersected with the politically opportune issue of the death penalty. The legislation was unique in that it stated that the Sentencing Commission was an independent commission *in the judicial branch*.

In 1987 and 1988, while we were still riding high from the 7–2 victory in the Gramm-Rudman case, defendants sentenced under the guidelines brought a large number of constitutional challenges in the district courts. The district judges hated the guidelines: not just because they were intricate and hard to apply, but because the discretion of sentencing judges was one of the few examples of virtually unreviewable power in our legal system. The defense lawyers also hated the guidelines, which meant stiffer sentences and less to bargain over.

The grounds for these constitutional challenges varied from the absurd[61] to the serious.[62] Since these challenges were all in the district courts, the Solicitor General had no formal say in how they would be answered. The Office of Legal Counsel, however, used them as an occasion to further the geometric conception of the separation of powers. True, the Department had participated in the negotiations leading up the Act, and President Reagan had signed it. But OLC was less interested in regularizing sentences than in the philosophical and constitutional issues. In their heart of hearts I suspect they felt the Act was unconstitutional, and they were willing to see a defense go forward only on the most limited terms. As far as OLC was concerned, the guidelines would be defended as an exercise of executive power—in spite of the words of the Act which lodged the Commission in the Judicial Branch—or it would not be defended at all.

This provoked a ferocious battle between the Commission and the Department. The Chairman and the most influential members of the Commission were all judges, and they resented any suggestion that they were now part of the Executive Branch as well as any aspersions cast on their independence. The episode with the death-penalty proposals was seen as just a taste of what it would be like to be embroiled in Executive Branch politics and projects. OLC responded by taking the position that the Commission, as an Executive Branch agency, could only be represented in court by the Department of Justice—with the Department controlling the substance of the legal arguments. A compromise was reached: the Commission would present its own theory of the Act in its own name by its own lawyers, but only as a friend of the court.

The Commission hired Paul Bator, who immediately took a different position from that of the Department. The court arguments—especially a dramatic argument before the Ninth Circuit Court of Appeals—became three-cornered fights: defendants arguing the invalidity of the Act on any terms, the Department arguing the Act's validity only if the Commission were (contrary to the words of the statute) viewed as being part of the Executive Branch, and Bator arguing for the validity of the scheme exactly as written.

The case was a perfect vehicle for Bator to put forward Justice White's thesis about the separation of powers. In fact, because this was an independent agency supposed to be in the Judicial Branch, Bator had even greater scope for his general thesis that

> Congress [has] . . . explicit constitutional authority . . . to determine how *all* the branches of government should be organized. . . . The Constitution does not spell out a detailed table of organization. . . . Rather, the Constitution leaves broad latitude to Congress to decide what institutions, and what allocations of subsidiary and interstitial responsibilities, will best carry out the constitutional plan for the other branches of government.[63]

If Congress could now grant rule-making powers to independent agencies, and for the first time lodge those powers within the *Judicial* Branch, then the authority of the President over the execution of the laws could be radically fractured, scattered, and diminished. OLC was right to see in the Act a threat to our conception of the separation of powers.

But in the summer of 1988, when the time came for us to prepare our defense of the Sentencing Reform Act in the Supreme Court, the Independent Counsel case had just been decided, and I concluded that the Department's separation-of-powers initiative was dead. The matter was firmly in my hands, because it was a Supreme Court brief and I would argue the case. I believed there were two realistic goals: first, to try to save the guidelines, which represented a major victory of the Reagan administration in terms of substantive policy; and, second, to minimize the damage to separation-of-powers principles that might be done in the course of winning the substantive battle. I also feared that an open battle between the Solicitor General and Paul Bator before the Supreme Court would give those attacking the guidelines their best chance at defeating them. I tried to persuade the Commission to back off and present a common front with us.

My line was that it did not much matter what the statute said about the "location" of the Commission. The Constitution, after all, does not speak of branches but, rather, of powers. And it was agreed on all sides that the Commission, since it is not passing on individual cases, was not exercising judicial power. The question of "location" then becomes merely a convenient device both for asserting the independence of the Commission from the President and for making certain housekeeping arrangements of no constitutional significance. I would not push the presidential prerogatives over the Commission, if the Commission would back off from using this as an occasion to establish the White-Bator position. I did succeed in getting the Commission to tone down its brief a little—particularly by refraining from attacking the Department's position as such—but as the above passage shows, the heart of the Bator thesis beat on every page.

Still, I was determined not to make an issue of the impingement on executive prerogatives but, rather, to concentrate on defending the Act against the charges that it was improper to delegate such broad and important powers to *anyone* and that it was improper to use judges on the Commission. By this time (the fall of 1988) Attorney General Meese had resigned and been replaced by Dick Thornburgh. The fiercest proponents of presidential power, John Bolton in the Civil Division and Doug Kmiec, who had taken over from Chuck Cooper in OLC, knew that their days in the Department were numbered, and they were determined to make one last stand for the "muscular" and "unitary" presidency. I was not. I could read. I had read the Independent Counsel case. I wanted to save the guidelines. Bolton and Kmiec made an eleventh-hour appeal against my strategy to the Attorney General, who did not wave me off. In fact, Attorney General Thornburgh, whom I had just introduced to the Court (as is customary on the first day of the term), the next day came to the argument and sat with me throughout. As a former United States Attorney, a former head of the Criminal Division, and a tough law-and-order man, he obviously cared a great deal about this reform of the criminal law.

The argument went well, with most of the attention from the bench directed to the substantive fairness of the guidelines and to the propriety of having judges join in performing extrajudicial functions.[64] The issue that had had the Department and the Commission at each other's throats for over a year scarcely came up.

The Court sustained the Act by a vote of 8–1. The opinion was a disaster. Justice Blackmun had been assigned the opinion by the Chief Justice, and he accepted the heart of the Bator brief—indeed, portions were incorporated in the opinion. Only Justice Scalia dissented. His dissent was one of his finest. He located the principal vice of the Act exactly at the place where I chose to defend it: the delegation—to whomsoever—of this authority away from the legislature.

> The whole theory of lawful congressional "delegation" is not that Congress is sometimes too busy or too divided and can therefore assign its responsibility of making law to someone else; but rather that a certain degree of discretion, and thus of law-making, inheres in most executive or judicial action, and it is up to Congress, by the relative specificity or generality of its statutory commands, to determine—up to a point—how small or how large that degree shall be.
>
> . . . Strictly speaking, there is no acceptable delegation of legislative power. . . . In the present case, however, a pure delegation of legislative power is precisely what we have before us. It is irrelevant whether the standards are adequate, because they are not standards related to the exercise of executive or judicial powers; they are, plainly and simply, standards for further legislation. . . .
>
> . . .
>
> I think the Court errs, in other words, not so much because it mistakes the degree of commingling, but

169

because it fails to recognize that this case is not about commingling, but about the creation of a new branch altogether, a sort of junior-varsity Congress. It may well be that in some circumstances such a branch would be desirable; perhaps the agency before us here will prove to be so. But there are many desirable dispositions that do not accord with the constitutional structure we live under. And in the long run the improvisation of a constitutional structure on the basis of currently perceived utility will be disastrous.[65]

If by sacrificing the guidelines Justice Scalia's opinion could have been made to become the opinion of the Court, it would have been worth it. But I know of no way this could have been done. Instead the Sentencing-Guidelines case was bound to become another nail in the coffin of a rigorous view of the separation of powers. Whether the coffin is nailed up tight I cannot say, but I am not optimistic.

I doubt that the ground we lost can be retrieved in this Court. Perhaps we could never have got the Supreme Court to announce as a theorem of constitutional law the picture of the separation of powers I have been painting: a governmental organization clear, accountable, and effective, moved by the principles of liberty, the rule of law, and the transparency of power. The vision I offer is not literally required by the words of the Constitution. Nor did the framers' intent compel this view. No, that vision must be discerned from the structure of the document as a whole, the logic implicit in the arrangement of its parts. Most of all, it is a vision based on the best and most compelling extrapolation from what was written in that text, what was said about it, and what was dreamed of by those who inspired it. These are arguments unlikely to impress the literal-minded temper of the present Court. They are arguments like the one that led to Justice Harlan's dissent in *Poe* v. *Ullman* and to the right of privacy—but also to *Roe* v. *Wade*. Justice Holmes said of such arguments, in his dissent in an earlier separation-of-powers case, that they are "spider's webs inadequate to control the dominant facts."[66] But a spider's web has a beautiful symmetry, a perfect logic.

6

LOYALTY

Certainly, Gentlemen, it ought to be the happiness and glory of a representative to live in the strictest union, the closest correspondence, and the most unreserved communication with his constituents. Their wishes ought to have great weight with him; their opinion high respect; their business unremitting attention. It is his duty to sacrifice his repose, his pleasure, his satisfaction, to theirs—and above all, ever, to prefer their interest to his own.

But his unbiased opinion, his mature judgment, his enlightened conscience, he ought not to sacrifice to you, to any man, or to any set of men living. . . .[1]

*B*y firing his officers, a President shows he means it about the separation of powers, about the unitary executive, about presidential prerogatives—in much the same way that letting bankruptcies happen shows you are serious about the discipline of the market. If the President is entitled to make his will prevail within his establishment, don't we, his "principal officers," have a corresponding duty to bend our intelligence and effort to the most subtle and accurate ascertainment of that will? Should we not try to extend and multiply that will into every corner of the Executive Branch? If decisiveness in command is a virtue in the chief, then it would seem that loyalty is the corresponding virtue of the subordinate officer. Yet there is a real issue about what loyalty to his President means in the case of a high government official.

There are two concepts available. One would have the officer put himself so far as possible in the President's shoes, trying to guess what the chief would do if he had the matter before him. The other—let us call it the Burkean view—sees loyalty as essentially an interpretive virtue according to which the officer uses his own judgment and values to make the best and most coherent whole out of his administration's projects and tendencies.

This distinction is illustrated by a story Victor Navasky tells in his book, *Kennedy Justice.* An earlier Solicitor General and former Harvard professor, Archibald Cox, faced a conflict between the technical but crucial constitutional doctrine of state action and the Kennedy administration's desire to use the courts, rather than a recalcitrant Congress, to ban segregation at private lunch counters and other such places— segregation which had given rise to some of the civil-rights movement's most dramatic confrontations. The Constitution states that "no state . . . shall deny any person . . . the equal protection of the law"—that is, discriminate. It required quite a stretch to say that when a private store-owner kept blacks off his property this was an instance of the *state's* discriminating, and (except in one case involving state enforcement of racist restrictive covenants[2]) the Supreme Court had held fast to the distinction between private and governmental action, applying the equal-protection guarantees only to the latter. Cox, like his mentor Justice Felix Frankfurter, believed that both the text and the integrity of the constitutional scheme required holding fast to this distinction. The Kennedy Justice Department was eager to break down this distinction and so to get the courts to do the work in eliminating segregation which it could not get out of Congress—not until after JFK's death and the Civil Rights Act of 1964.

> The liberal view, put forth by men like Jack Greenberg, the . . . chief counsel of the NAACP Inc. Fund . . . was that in today's complex world it made little sense to talk about "state action" in the narrow meaning of that term. . . . [Greenberg felt] that regardless of what one believed to be the better theoretical position, the law was in flux and therefore the Solicitor should not decide such an issue on the basis of legal theory but rather on the basis of departmental policy. Greenberg, who had been invited to the Justice Department to air his opinions on the state-action issue, once told Cox, "If you believe your position, write it up for the Harvard Law Review. But now you're the Solicitor General of the United States, and it is the policy of the Kennedy Administration to oppose discrimination wherever it can."[3]

As I show later, Solicitor General Wade McCree came under much the same kind of pressure to adjust the conclusions of his loyal best judgment in order to make the government's brief in the *Bakke* case better accord with the administration's policy on affirmative action—at least that is how Joe Califano saw it. But the episode in my own tenure that best illustrates the two conflicting conceptions of loyalty was remarkably similar to the story of Cox's confrontation with Jack Greenberg. For me too the crux was fighting against an overly expansive view of the state-action doctrine—this time what I resisted was the notion that the First Amendment's prohibition against *government* restriction on freedom of speech extended to protect union members from the imperatives of private-sector labor unions.

Beck: Siding with the Union Bosses

It is not surprising that the state-action doctrine should be a source of tension. If an administration can get the Court to declare that some policy of that administration to regulate private conduct is really a matter of constitutional right, it gets the Court to do its political work for it. In my case, *Communications Workers of America* v. *Beck,*[4] the underlying political issue was the use of union dues and fees to support candidates and parties—inevitably, pro-union candidates and more often than not left-liberal causes. Unions and employers would often negotiate agreements that required workers to pay these fees in order to keep their jobs, whether or not they agreed with the politics the fees were used to support, and whether or not the workers joined the union. The

National Labor Relations Act (the 1935 Wagner Act, importantly modified in 1947 by the Taft-Hartley Act[5]) regulates and protects the status of a union with majority support as the sole representative of all the workers in a workplace. And this act had always been understood to permit unions to enforce these kinds of forced contributions. The practice is deeply offensive.[6] It reeks of the anti-individualistic, corporatist mentality that characterized the early New Deal.[7] The practice was condemned in the 1980 and 1984 Republican platforms. And it appears that the President himself, who may have been influenced by his early experience in the Screen Actors Guild, disliked this practice. (Some unions, like the UAW, shared this dislike, and for years have offered a rebate to objecting dues-payers.)

The National Labor Relations Board (NLRB) is the independent agency that oversees the labor laws. Since the beginning of the Reagan administration, the Right to Work Legal Foundation—whose leaders, Rex Reed and Reed Larson, were among the most hard-line "movement" conservatives—had been trying to get the NLRB to adopt either an interpretation of the labor laws or a Board policy banning the political use of compelled union dues. The Board refused to do this. So when the *Beck* case came up and the Supreme Court requested the views of the United States about whether the labor acts allowed the political use of union dues and, if it did, whether this violated the Constitution, the stage seemed at last to be set for a showdown. Making our pitch to the Court—rather than to the Board or to Congress, where it was sure to fail—seemed particularly promising. A quarter of a century before, in the *Street* case,[8]

Justice Brennan, writing for a sharply divided Supreme Court, had issued such a ban against the compelled political use of union dues under the similar but not identical scheme of the Railway Labor Act—an act that governs the railroad and airline industries.[9]

Because the case was such a hot one, I again set up a formal procedure, by which the contending parties—the AFL/CIO and Right to Work—would argue to me and my staff what position the SG should take before the Court. The Right to Work presentation focused almost entirely on the Constitution. The First Amendment protected not only against laws that would silence you, but also against laws that made you speak against your will, particularly against laws that made you support positions at odds with your political or religious convictions. This principle had been the basis of the flag-salute case, but more recently had been used to protect government employees from political exactions by public-employee unions with which governments struck bargains requiring the payment of union fees.[10] If public employees and railroad workers are protected from such exactions, should not the rest of the unionized work force be protected also?

The crux was state action. The First Amendment protects only against government restrictions on speech. The Constitution does not prevent a teacher at a private university from being muzzled, or a newspaper publisher from controlling what the editorial writers say. In fact, the opposite is closer to being true: freedom of speech is thought to be protected when private institutions are free to control the speech for which they are responsible. This is a profoundly liberal view of the First Amendment, and it distresses communitarians on the left as well as on the right. Extremists on both wings join in decrying the ability of powerful private institutions (the media, universities, labor unions) to control public debate, and wave aside the state-action requirement as a lawyers' quibble.

The Right to Work argument was more subtle. According to them, the union's exaction was backed by the government and therefore had a sufficient aspect of state action about it. The national labor laws protected and privileged the status of the majority union. The Board supervised and certified the election designating the majority union, and from then on the law gave it a monopoly status as the exclusive bargaining agent for the whole work unit.[11] This government-assured monopoly was the real target of the Right to Work argument. They saw it as an offense to what they took to be the constitutional right of everyone to make whatever arrangements he chose to find work or workers. The Supreme Court had once entertained this argument, but had rejected it half a century before in the general demise of the *Lochner* doctrine.[12] But this counterrevolutionary attempt to revive *Lochner*, which had some partisans among the Attorney General's assistants, wore a more reasonable aspect here. The argument sought to draw enough state involvement from the union's government-assured monopoly status to overcome the state-action hurdle and so subject union contracts with private employers to the First Amendment.

I could not accept this argument, or commit the administration to it. In my constitutional catechism, the line between the public and the private must be drawn firmly. And in recent years the Supreme Court had held the line—Chief Justice Rehnquist writing the strongest opinions,[13] and Justice Brennan invariably in dissent. If the welfare-bureaucratic state's various involvements in private institutions became a basis for subjecting those institutions to the same constitutional provisions as bear on the state, the way would be open to impose on every institution in the country the same leveling and intrusive regimes as are now imposed (often quite properly) on the government alone. And the way would be open as well to regulate the private sector not by legislation alone (we have quite enough of that), but by ideologically aggressive lawyers and a creative judiciary.[14] In my view, the mere fact that a business corporation or a private university receives a state charter or participates in a government program, or even gets a government contract, does not mean that it should therefore be seen as subject to the Fourteenth Amendment, or that its officers should be liable to suit under Section 1983 of the Civil Rights Act, or that it could not maintain a chapel and chaplains. In this respect, history did seem to repeat itself, only with Right to Work pressing Jack Greenberg's line of analysis.

The other argument in support of the *result* that Right to Work, the President, and I all preferred was that the Taft-Hartley Act could be read as forbidding the political use of compulsory dues. This seemed to me not unprincipled—as was the constitutional point —but disingenuous. In the clearest terms, the language of Taft-Hartley excludes internal union affairs and issues regarding union dues from its scope of inquiry.[15] And if this were not enough, the legislative history also speaks directly to the issue. The House version of the bill did indeed contain a provision prohibiting this use of union dues, but in conference Senator Taft himself successfully urged its removal. He explained that the Congress was looking at a sure veto by President Truman and that in order to save the most important provisions—the prohibitions on secondary boycotts and on closed shops—it was necessary to recede from some of the peripheral restrictions of this House bill.[16] None of us who worked on the brief could see how we could disregard the text or this clear expression of legislative intent—at least not without engaging in the same kind of Houdini-like interpretive magic that Justice Rehnquist accused Justice Brennan of working in the *Weber* case (and which Justice Brennan had worked two decades earlier to force his interpretation on the Railway Labor Act in *Street*).

So, in answering the question the Court put to the Solicitor General, I had to face the music—neither the Constitution nor the labor acts prevented the Communications Workers from using Harry Beck's union dues to support candidates and causes he didn't like. Our nominal client was the Labor Board. Though on this occasion their preferences were quite irrelevant to my conclusions, we circulated the galley proofs of our brief to them for their comments. Along the line someone sent them to the White House, and all hell broke loose. As protocol requires, whoever was unhappy over there got in touch with the Attorney General through his Counselor Brad Reynolds. Brad understood completely my constitutional scruples and shared them—as did Chuck Cooper, whom he generally consulted on these things. After all, Chuck had clerked for Chief Justice Rehnquist, who was principally responsible for holding the line on the state-action doctrine. Others were less impressed with the brief. John Bolton, head of Legislative Affairs, told me that Republicans in Congress were furious when they heard what the Solicitor General was about to file in Court. I told him that if he could come up with an analysis that could turn me around I would be delighted. Attorney General Meese's reaction was typical. He called a general meeting in which anyone who had a view on the issue (even if this was not at all in his area of responsibility) had his say. By now the brief was printed and bound, but he asked me to hear everyone out and answer all the objections. The attacks in the Department and in the White House, it seemed, focused on the statutory analysis. And at a later stage Brad Reynolds told me quite matter-of-factly that I would do myself a lot of good if I could find my way clear to proposing a reading of the labor laws that would bar the political use of union dues. He was not trying to pressure me; this was a piece of information it was his duty to pass on. Finally, at the last possible moment, Meese asked whether I was really sure of my ground; only then did the brief go up to the Court.

Right to Work was beside itself with fury. Their newsletter berated me and sought to raise ten-dollar donations from the faithful to combat my piece of treachery in unspecified ways. I got bushels of letters from their membership. *Human Events* devoted its front page to a story with the headline "Key Justice Official Sides with Union Bosses."[17] One bit of speculation had it that the administration had sold out in exchange for union backing for Contra aid. And I read that one of Harry Beck's lawyers claimed he had "button-holed the President" to complain about my position before the Supreme Court and that " 'The President said he was absolutely furious with [Fried's] decision.' "[18] Nor was this quite the end of the story. Rex Reed and Reed Larson approached the Attorney General just before the case was to be argued to demand that I be ordered to withdraw our brief. Meese set up a meeting with them and asked me to be there too. We heard them out and thanked them very much. Here was another parallel to the meeting at which Jack Greenberg had come into the Justice Department to harangue Archie Cox.

Only the outcome was different. My analysis was rejected. Mr. Beck and Right to Work won. Taft-Hartley was "construed" to prohibit the use of union dues for political purposes to avoid what were called grave constitutional difficulties. Justice Brennan wrote for the Court, and only Justices Blackmun, O'Connor, and Scalia dissented.

Did I not fail here in my duty to my political superiors? Should I not have taken the clear indication of presidential concern as my guide? After all, in the event, it could hardly be said that the White House position was unreasonable; it had prevailed in the Supreme Court by a vote of 5–3.

Property Rights, Economic Liberty, and Federalism

For me the most severe tests of loyalty, the incidents that tested not just character but judgment, did not have to do with calls to act unlawfully or to violate some specific undertaking. Rather, the most difficult tests came when my political superiors wanted me to press positions in the Supreme Court that accorded with reasonable and legitimate principles I did not share, or to which I did not give the same priority as they did. *Beck* was not such a case. I was convinced that mine was a more faithful reading of what was at the heart of my administration's philosophy. These other, hard cases had to do with relatively obscure and technical protections for property rights.

Certainly economic liberty, deregulation, and the fight against unprincipled, ad-hoc, sentimental redistributive adjudication in the federal courts were among the projects that had brought me to government and the administration in the first place. But Attorney General Meese and his young advisers— many drawn from the ranks of the then fledgling Federalist Societies and often devotees of the extreme libertarian views of Chicago law professor Richard Epstein—had a specific, aggressive, and, it seemed to me, quite radical project in mind: to use the Takings Clause of the Fifth Amendment as a severe brake upon federal and state regulation of business and property.[19] The grand plan was to make government pay compensation as for a taking of property every time its regulations impinged too severely on a property right—limiting the possible uses for a parcel of land or restricting or tying up a business in regulatory red tape. If the government labored under so severe an obligation, there would be, to say the least, much less regulation. The immediate issue concerned a nasty little trick that the overzealous land regulators in California and their allies in the state Supreme Court (then headed by Chief Justice Rose Bird) had devised. The trick allowed land regulators to go as far as they dared in regulating land, and then, if they had overstepped constitutional boundaries and committed a taking even under existing constitutional doctrine, they could avoid compensating the landowner by just giving up on the proposed restriction after perhaps years of litigation and a vast destruction of his economic interest.[20] The Attorney General, who was from California and had many friends who were involved in local California land battles, was personally committed to squelching this practice.

The first step in the takings battle would be to say that, if the landowner ultimately prevailed, he was constitutionally entitled to compensation for his losses during the whole time his interests had been tied up by the excessive regulation. This proposition was called the interim-damages thesis. It made me very nervous. It was not my usual role as a lawyer for the government to devise doctrines that would impede government action and end up costing the government money—those arguments could be made by private parties. But that was an objection I would readily ignore if I had been sure the argument was correct on its merits.

It was the merits that bothered me. I doubted the wisdom of giving the courts a powerful new engine for redistributing to sympathetic plaintiffs possibly vast sums of money at the expense of the public. I was alerted to the danger by the fact that Justice Brennan had once expressed sympathy for the interim-damages argument.[21] I was quite right to suppose that Justice Brennan was not particularly moved by the concerns of businesses and property owners who were unfairly put upon by overzealous regulators.[22] Here as always I supposed he was moved by his overriding egalitarian philosophy, by a concern to protect the "new property," to secure the expectations of welfare beneficiaries, government-job holders, and the like.[23] The doctrine of interim damages, if promoted to constitutional status, could have the effect of constitutionalizing to an unpredictable extent large portions of the welfare state. And this was the dream of many constitutional scholars on the left.[24] Loyal to what I conceived to be the heart of the Reagan Revolution, I thought that tax cuts and budget reductions were the only effective and systematic way to control the leveling tendencies of the welfare state.[25] To fixate on episodic though admittedly galling impositions on individual landowners seemed to me a distraction hardly worth the systematic risks a "victory" might entail.

So I fought to avoid filing a brief in support of the landowners in the two cases raising this issue.[26] I explained my reluctance in several memos and meetings, but it was clear the Attorney General was quite determined. After an all-night drafting session, I even expressed to my Counselor Carolyn Kuhl a desperate wish to quit over the whole thing. Her response was wise and correct: "Jeeze Louise, quit over a Mickey Mouse thing like this?" In the end, I achieved a compromise: We proposed that, if government officials tied up the property owner in unduly complicated or protracted procedures to adjudicate the takings claims, this harassment would make the officials liable for violating the property owner's constitutional right to due process of law. But there would not also be an automatic right to interim damages, nor yet a right to damages from the government itself. I compromised because I agreed with Carolyn about the relative unimportance of the issue, but also because in fact the Attorney General (like Brad Reynolds in the aftermath of *Stotts*) had good legal authority on his side. It would be an indefensible reversal of role for the Solicitor General to go to the mat in the name of general policy while the Attorney General had the better of the technical legal argument. In the event, the Supreme Court, in an opinion by Chief Justice Rehnquist, dismissed my halfway proposals in a footnote[27] and adopted the Attorney General's full-blooded position. My prediction that this would be used against the government in a welfare-rights case was soon realized. In *Schweiker* v. *Chilicky*[28] my colleague Larry Tribe, against whom I argued the case, made full use of the proposition the Court had just adopted,[29] but Chief Justice Rehnquist, again writing for the Court, did not accept the analogy from a landowner's to a welfare recipient's case. I won the case, and Justice Brennan dissented.

A disagreement over the principle of federalism led me into a very similar conflict with the Attorney General and many colleagues in the Department— especially Chuck Cooper and Brad Reynolds.[30] They sought every possible way to redress the balance of power between the federal and local governments, which had shifted in the last half-century to favor the national government overwhelmingly. Their project had a convinced and important ally in President Reagan. The driving force behind their argument was the belief, widely held in the generation that had framed and ratified the Constitution, that strong local institutions were a bulwark of democracy and a protection against impositions by an arrogant, distant, and over-reaching national government. I was not so sure. I feared the "village tyrant," an equally serious threat to individual liberty. Localism was a potentially virulent source of Luddite and leveling impositions. My perspective was no doubt sharpened by years of living in the People's Republic of Cambridge, which, together with Berkeley, California, has one of the most stringent and stupid rent-control schemes in the country, along with a host of other extreme schemes and policies on all kinds of inappropriate subjects. I would regularly make myself unpopular at the Attorney General's meetings by pointing out that local affirmative-action and racial set-aside ordinances were a perfect illustration of my concerns, and one that the administration agreed ought to be subject to severe federal restrictions.

One form the federalism project took was to seek to "direct" the Department's lawyers to argue for a presumption that congressional regulatory schemes did not displace local schemes on the same subject, unless Congress had spoken with an unmistakable clarity of which it was rarely capable. This seemed to me a disastrous idea. At a time when the federal government was committed to loosening the regulations that hampered economic efficiency, political entrepreneurs would be let loose at the local level, at the expense of the public and of consumers. Better that firms operating on a national basis be subject to one uniform system of regulation than to scores of different ones. In a fractured and uncoordinated situation, businesses would as a practical matter be forced to comply with whatever regulations were most stringent. I argued and I resisted. My work was subject to scrutiny by the federalism police, and I was pulled over more than once and issued federalism speeding tickets. But in the end I had to yield a good bit of ground, because the federalists got the President to issue a federalism Executive Order.[31] Although that order included an escape hatch I had drafted, and was addressed only to the conduct of federal agencies and not to how I argued cases in the Supreme Court, I felt that an unduly grudging response to a formal and authoritative presidential order would be improper and disloyal.[32] Of course I must admit that I did not quite take this project so entirely to my heart that I made it readily and instinctively my own. Indeed, I was probably guilty of some considerable backsliding in the last big fight I had with the federalism police, involving the Solicitor General's position in *Amerada Hess* v. *New Jersey*,[33] a case dealing with state taxation of interstate business. I received my rebuke in a unanimous decision by the Supreme Court.

Two Concepts of Loyalty

One of the conceptions of loyalty that I have identified might be called the political-science or mandate conception.[34] According to this view, an officer's or representative's duty is to discern accurately the wishes and interests of his chief or his constituency, then to sum these up according to their number and intensity, and finally to implement them shrewdly and effectively. The political entrepreneur, insufficiently adept at reading the political market's signals and responding to them, will be put out of business— that is, voted out of office. And so too a political appointee will undertake to serve the passions of his political superior, the President. If he fails to discern them aright, or implements them clumsily, he will be replaced; otherwise he will be rewarded with promotion and praise.

This conception is quite wrong. It completely misses what is at stake for a legislator or an appointed official. I owed loyalty to the President and to my superior in the Department of Justice, the Attorney General. Such loyalty is enjoined both by law and by a proper conception of the President's establishment; it is a matter neither of affection nor of self-interest. It is a moral attitude; the object of this loyalty must be recognized as having intrinsic value, as being worth following for its own sake and in principle. First we judge a thing or a person to be worthy of our loyalty, and then—and for that reason—subordinate our will to it. That is why loyalty makes for dependability, since our choices are determined as long as our minds hold to the same judgment; and that is why disloyalty is also seen as unprincipled, since when we are disloyal we allow a lesser or a private good to determine our action. As Josiah Royce expressed it, loyalty gives a steadfastness of bearing and implies a seriousness of judgment.[35]

The President is entitled to loyalty conceived in just this way from those he appoints to high office. It is not the entitlement of gratitude, although those who would be more properly charged with disloyalty are often accused of ingratitude. Gratitude would be owed if the President bestowed office as a personal favor—but the President is owed loyalty as the reciprocal of the authority he wields in our constitutional system. He should be able to enforce obedience by firing his officers, and they owe him loyalty so that his projects may be executed not grudgingly but with imagination and firmness. A President can expect loyalty from his political appointees because they are chosen to share his particular project for the country, a project to which they may expect that he will be as loyal as he is.

It follows that the political-science or mandate view is wrong in its explanation of the duties of office, as it is wrong in its explanation of the duty of elected representatives. The officer is loyal to his chief in principle, not as a rule of thumb for getting, holding, or rising in office. The "unbiased opinion," "mature judgment," and "enlightened conscience" are the independent conclusions of principle that thoughtful men and women come to in choosing the leaders and causes to which they give loyalty.

In appointing an officer, the President chooses not an instrument but a person. This measures what the President can expect, and what his officers owe in the way of loyalty. It would be absurd to equate the rather dry and obscure issues of the *Beck* case with the high issues of conscience and politics that provoked the important resignations of the past: William Jennings Bryan's resignation over Wilson's war policy, Henry Wallace's break with Truman over Truman's reversal of the Roosevelt policy of accommodating Stalin, Cyrus Vance's resignation after the failed hostage-rescue mission, or the wonderful history of tempestuous resignations in Great Britain, from Lord Randolph Churchill's resignation from Salisbury's government, through his son Winston's resignation in 1915, and Eden's and Bevan's and a dozen other such gestures.[36]

Though obscure and not particularly important (especially since the Court ignored my submission), the *Beck* episode illustrates these questions of loyalty.

My decision was certainly disloyal from the political-science view: those whom I represented were displeased with it. Yet, from another viewpoint, I served them loyally. I believed the constitutional principles and principles of interpretive integrity were far closer to the heart of what the administration had proclaimed as its program than the issue of the political use of union dues.[37] I acted as if I knew the President's mind on this matter better than he did himself—on the principle that I was chosen as Solicitor General not because the President had a view and a policy about all of the detailed and technical matters I would have to deal with, but because he had a general disposition about the law, about the Constitution, about how courts ought to work.[38] I shared that disposition, but had a scholar's and specialist's vantage—I knew what it meant better than a layman and generalist would.

I had been appointed to exercise my judgment, rather than to try to guess what Ronald Reagan would have said about some particular technical matter. Indeed, the last is quite literally a nonsensical criterion for judgment. Public office is an interpretive activity. The officer tries to make the best sense out of his assignment. He must judge how to make a coherent morally and politically good whole out of his political superior's directives, pronouncements, hints, and actions.[39]

Is this a conception that leaves far too much to the willful and perhaps disloyal officer—allowing him the comfort of calling what he does loyalty into the bargain? And how may a superior rein in a rogue subordinate? There is, of course, dismissal—but that is a most drastic and perhaps ineffective way of bringing coherence to the executive establishment. The more obvious method would be to issue a direct order. But there is a problem about that in most situations in American national politics. As was the case with Andrew Jackson's Secretary of the Treasury Duane, most officers of the United States carry out duties in their own name, and the duties they carry out cannot be discharged personally by the President even if he wants to do so. The President could not have submitted a brief in the *Beck* case, since the law provides that (with certain limited exceptions) only the Attorney General or the Solicitor General may submit (or authorize the submission of) a brief in the name of the United States before the Supreme Court.[40] So, if the Solicitor General chose not to obey the President's order, the President would have to fire him and find a successor to carry out the order. This is what happened not only to Duane, but to Richardson and Ruckelshaus. The President's power to dismiss Executive Branch officers should be even clearer than it already is, but, assuming he has the power, is it disloyal on the part of the officer to force the President to use it?

Resign!

If an order requires a violation of law, it must not be obeyed—even a common soldier gains no immunity and has no privilege to obey an illegal order. If the order is only arguably illegal—that is, a good lawyer might make a case on either side—but the officer believes the order illegal, the conclusion is still the same. An ordinary advocate, however, is entirely free to propose to a court legal arguments on behalf of his client that as a judge he would reject. But an officer of the government—even a legal officer like the Solicitor General—is not just like this ordinary advocate in someone else's cause. He is the principal. It is his cause, just as an officer of a corporation cannot hide behind the lawyer's role but is personally responsible for what he does. As a legal officer of the government one does more than just propose arguments to a court. As Solicitor General I underwrote them— proposed them *as correct.* In the case of an improper order, then, loyalty requires resignation: it would not be right for the officer to disregard the President and make him take the initiative to fire him. To put oneself at odds with one's superior and then continue to act in his name suggests an entitlement to office which no unelected person has.

And how do you resign? Do you threaten to resign and then carry out the threat? Do you make your reasons public? And how? It is farfetched to imagine a situation in which an officer is ordered to do something he considers illegal without first having a chance to tell the President that this is how he judges the matter. If an officer is dealt with so abruptly, then an abrupt resignation is all the President is entitled to—and probably all he would be interested in. More usually, anything as categorical as an order would be preceded by discussions and consultation. In these the officer has an obligation to make plain that he thinks a planned course of action would be wrong. And if the President still insists, he cannot be surprised if his order precipitates a resignation accompanied by a public statement giving the precise grounds for the resignation. At the early stages of a project, of course, many people seek to soften conflict, to put issues of principle as matters of judgment and strategy so as not to seem priggish. But that kind of evasion carries a real risk. If you have not made the grounds of your disagreement clear beforehand, it is dishonorable to increase the stakes unilaterally when your superior is already committed on a set of assumptions you helped to evoke. Then you are truly in a hard spot, with no one but yourself to blame. In such a case, the mumbled excuse about ill health or a desire to return to private life is about all you are entitled to.

But illegal orders are rare. In my four years in government I did not see one.[41] And few of the resignations in the chronicles of American or British Cabinet history have related to such orders.[42] The most celebrated resignations in our history came, rather, over deep disagreements on policy. William Jennings Bryan resigned as Secretary of State to protest Woodrow Wilson's war policy. And Henry Wallace's pro-Soviet views led him to leave Truman's Cabinet. He ran against Truman as a candidate of what Truman (with justified scorn) called the American Crackpots Association. Such resignations are common in Britain and should be more common in this country. The reluctance of American officials to resign has been attributed to an excessively subservient and careerist spirit,[43] but I think the causes go deeper.

American Cabinet or sub-Cabinet officers are constitutionally creatures of appointment. Though the Senate must confirm them, there is general agreement that the President is entitled to be served by his own people, as long as they are competent and honest. The British Cabinet officer comes from Parliament and on resignation returns to it, so that he has an elected political status in principle no different from that of his leader. The American official on resigning loses not only his ministerial power but any public role. He does not explain his resignation in the House or retain a seat there, as did Churchill throughout most of his wilderness years. He becomes an instant outsider. Thus, the American officer rightly feels he is the President's servant. The Prime Minister is only the first of the Queen's several ministers.

Yet I think we have drawn the wrong conclusion from this undoubted fact. It seems to me to require, if anything, a greater readiness to resign,[44] since presidential decisions are neither in form nor in substance the collective decisions of the Cabinet. (There is the famous tale of Lincoln polling his Cabinet and announcing that the vote was ten against, one for: "The ayes have it.") The President and only the President has been elected, and indeed is the only person elected by the whole country, to lead. But if my account of loyalty is correct, this means that the President not merely deserves to be, but can only be effectively served by officers whose minds, in the words of Franklin Roosevelt's letter to FTC Commissioner Humphrey, "go along together" with his. That can only mean that what the officer conceives in his particular domain, as a result of his own independent judgment, extends and enlarges and conforms to the President's will. It is not at all a matter of guessing the President's mind—for he is unlikely to have one on the matter—but of constructing his leader's mind in a way that he will later embrace as his own.

The direct order is problematic, not because it impugns the independence and dignity of the officer but, rather, because the very necessity for it is the sign that there is a discordance between the officer and the chief. If it is necessary to force the officer's subservience, it is not only demeaning, but also a symptom of a relationship that is not what it should be. But an independent concordance cannot be easily attained or maintained, and therefore I would guess we should have had many more resignations than we have actually seen.

In contrast, the whole conception of a civil service, protected from political considerations in hiring, promotion, and firing, is different from that of the politically appointed officer. The President would be in a poor situation indeed if all the millions of civil servants were entitled to personal and political autonomy (as are appointed political officers) and yet he could exercise no discretion in choosing or keeping them. If the President were not entitled to have his own policy goals, and if all actions within his domain were determined by law, then the question of the loyalty of his agents would not come up—the only questions would be about their competence and conscientiousness. And that is the conception that some enthusiasts for congressional government offer.[45] Since this conception is at odds with the independent constitutional role of the American President, there remains the need to understand the role of the career civil servant in the executive establishment.

That conception must acknowledge the high degree of judgment, experience, and esteem that civil servants claim. They are not mere clerical workers. Since they constitute the largest part of the Executive Branch and occupy all the posts except the handful at the top of each agency, their claims to respect had better be justified, or the public management of the country is in poor hands. The civil servant must accept policy direction from political superiors and must take their policies as his own. Neither the civil servant nor his superiors have a right to expect that their minds will "go along together." Unlike the political officer, the civil servant must be a policy chameleon, taking his coloration from the administration which he serves. The public business and the democratic principle, which authorizes the President's having a policy at all, are sufficient to remove any sense that the civil servant acts hypocritically. The personal dilemmas this creates can usually be accommodated. In the Solicitor General's office, for instance, we had a rule that no career lawyer would have to sign a brief about which he or she had conscientious scruples. We always respected that, and where the privilege was claimed, it was accorded without fuss.

In many agencies, particularly agencies that were set up all at once and with a specific mission, the civil servants often consider that it is they who are the true guardians of the agencies' goals, and that the political chiefs who come and go are interlopers, to be tolerated, humored, and, if they should really assert leadership, subverted—in the manner of the British political sitcom "Yes, Minister." With their detailed knowledge, their ties to congressional staffs and the press, and their network of associations with like-minded bureaucrats in other agencies, these civil servants are rightly described as making up a permanent government, beyond the reach of democratically elected and politically appointed chiefs. This phenomenon, however, is parasitic on the incompetence and timidity of political superiors. An able and confident political chief will both manage and protect his career staff. So here too the key is the independence and responsibility of that political officer.

As my own experience in *Beck* and the property rights and federalism cases shows, reality is often much more elusive than theory. In *Beck* I received no direct order. I was made aware that "the White House" did not like the position I was about to take. But it is one of the jokes of Washington how the lowliest of deputy special assistants to the President, operating out of a remote fourth-floor cubby in the Old Executive Office Building (an 1850s French Renaissance pile just west of the White House, sharing its perimeter fence) will telephone all over town, proclaiming portentously that "the White House" wants or thinks this or that. Of course an officer must act in his own name, and he should listen to all sorts of advice and opinions. And these opinions will sometimes be couched in peremptory and bullying language. What the officer should do—and I am not sure I succeeded sufficiently in *Beck*—is ignore the hectoring entirely and try to glean what might help his judgment: facts, arguments, connections to other policies he might not be aware of, connections to commitments he or his President has made. But it is a mistake to treat any of these interventions as having authoritative status; they are only as valid as their intrinsic weight. The President's federalism Executive Order was quite another matter— much more like a direct order.

As Solicitor General I had a statutory superior in the Attorney General, a superior whom by law I was designated to "assist" and who was formally competent (as the President, in mine and most other cases, is not) to do any act I could do. For that reason I took comfort from the fact that the Attorney General could formally overrule me—which is a little different from a direct order; it is more like what an appellate court does to a lower court. Whenever any of my colleagues in the administration—heads of Justice Department components, general counsels of other departments or agencies (client agencies), and once even a Cabinet Secretary—were dissatisfied with a ruling of mine, I invited them to carry an appeal to the Attorney General. It seemed to me that this freed me to take whatever position seemed right to me, while giving people a sense that a route of correction was open. It also clarified my relations to the Attorney General, since I could engage in all kinds of informal exchanges with him but still mark the point when I was making a final decision on my personal authority. If the Attorney General did not approve it, he could overrule it.[46]

As I read the accounts of other Solicitors General's major conflicts, I am not sure how they fit this model. I would suppose that Cox's accommodation with the Department's strong civil-rights commitments in arguing the unconstitutionality of enforcing private-lunch-counter segregation[47] might be seen as persuasion by eloquent voices. So perhaps might be his abandonment of his Frankfurterian scruples when he argued for the proposition that the Court should take on the issue of legislative apportionment. Those precedents suggest I was too stubborn (or unimaginative) in the *Beck* case. But, then, HEW Secretary Joseph Califano's account of how he orchestrated the pressure to change Solicitor General McCree's brief in *Bakke* to a position much more favorable to affirmative action leaves me with the sense that McCree (a fine and sensitively intelligent man) had been neither persuaded nor cleanly overruled, but just bullied—

though this may only be how Califano saw and reported the episode.[48]

Califano considered the Solicitor General's draft brief in the *Bakke* case to be a "chilling attack" on affirmative action. Califano proposed that he and his staff offer an alternative brief to the Attorney General and the President. There were numerous meetings with McCree, intervention by Stuart Eizenstat (Carter's chief domestic-policy adviser), and Vice-President Mondale. Partly at Califano's instigation, members of the Congressional Black Caucus tracked McCree down in Detroit in order to harangue him about the brief, which had been leaked to them. When the final product rejected the earlier draft's assertion that racial preferences were "presumptively unconstitutional," distinguished goals from quotas, and endorsed affirmative action, Califano pronounced himself satisfied. He telephoned Attorney General Griffin Bell to congratulate him. Bell complained that "We ended up with everyone in the government and the nation helping us write it." Califano thought this was "as it should be."[49]

When the *Bakke* case finally came down, Wade McCree must have felt the way I did in *Beck* or *First English*. The government's brief, over which he had suffered such pain, had culminated in this exchange with itself: "[We ask] whether a state university admissions program may take race into account to remedy the effects of societal discrimination. We submit that it may." Justice Powell's controlling opinion in *Bakke* and subsequent opinions for the Court have rejected that precise submission.

Califano's account of the *Bakke* episode also illustrates my point about civil servants.

[The] meeting . . . was deeply disturbing. McCree, who is black and had been a judge before he was appointed Solicitor General, sat with two bright young white holdovers from the Nixon administration. They did not disguise their distaste for affirmative action. . . .

I was surprised how angry I was becoming as the young lawyers spun their legalistic theories. McCree sat there, remarking simply that he had to follow existing case law, at times seeming to acquiesce in the arguments of his aides. . . .

One of McCree's lawyers thought it was impossible to write a brief that approved a special admissions policy [giving racial preferences].

"Like hell it's impossible," I said. "I don't have any problem writing it. . . . We are not going to have [the work of those who have worked for equality] thrown out the window by a couple of young lawyers."[50]

Something had gone terribly wrong in a meeting like that. The two "holdovers from the Nixon administration" were career civil servants. One of them, Lawrence Wallace, who had been hired in the last year of the Johnson administration by Solicitor General Erwin Griswold, had come in for at least as much abuse in the Reagan administration for his resistance to projects like *Bob Jones* and the *Guardians* case,[51] where he was very much a defender of affirmative action.* The scene lacks decorum. It is as if a guest in your home berated your cook for oversalting the soup. A famous and powerful Cabinet Secretary should not be getting into a shouting match with another officer's career staff. Political officers should never hide be-

* The other "holdover," Frank Easterbrook, became a professor at the University of Chicago Law School and is now a distinguished federal court-of-appeals judge. Both signed the brief McCree finally filed.

hind their staffs; and to the outside world staff members should have no opinions of their own. Their advice should be free and candid and expert, but given to their chief alone, who, if he accepts it, puts it forward on his own authority.

Go Quietly?

My account does leave some ambiguities. If I am overruled, who signs the brief—do I, or does the "appellate court," the Attorney General? And how often and in what depth is it tolerable to be overruled? There is something false about signing a brief containing views that you do not hold and on which you have been overruled.* Fortunately, the one explicit overruling I suffered, in *Wisconsin* v. *Gould,* concluded only that the brief we had drafted would not be submitted in the Solicitor General's name. To be overruled into silence is pretty nearly always tolerable. And, in general, some sense of proportion is necessary. Where the overruling is not on a crucial point, you should be willing to swallow and to take direction. It is only if you are asked to sign your name to a false or legally unfounded proposition, or one that offends important personal convictions, that you must balk— if for no other reason than that you are no longer acting as the kind of agent an officer of government should be. Certainly you may be wrong and the higher authority right, but if you cannot bring your-

---

* SG Perlman refused to sign the brief supporting the loyalty oath. It was submitted by Attorney General Brownell and Assistant Attorney General Warren Burger in *Peters* v. *Hobby,* 349 U.S. 331 (1955). Brownell later defended Perlman's loyalty, when Perlman was attacked in Senate confirmation hearings for a judgeship.

self into agreement, the conditions of confidence no longer exist that make collaboration appropriate. The same conclusion follows if as an officer you are overruled too often on more trivial matters.

This conclusion suggests answers to two other delicate questions—what do you say *before* you resign, and what do you say when you do resign? The whole time I was in government, I imposed on myself an iron rule against threatening resignation. If the time came when I was ordered to do what I felt I could not, or when there was no longer confidence between me and my administration, then I should just quit. Threatening resignation is coercive, and an officer has no right at all to seek to exert that kind of pressure on his administration. If the coercion works, it is only because the officer has attained an advantage over his superiors, and that is an advantage that comes from their trust in his loyalty. That trust does not require blind obedience, but neither should it be turned against those who trusted the officer.

By the same token, clamorous resignations designed to gain an advantage and destroy the policy you could not agree to, are also abusive. In the British tradition, the resigning Minister states his reasons pretty fully and forcefully to the House. But, again, that is a function of the fact that the resigning Minister remains a public person with a public function, and perhaps even a duty to report to his colleagues in the House.

Yet, if threatening resignation is wrong, is it not worse to allow your superior to walk into what he may later think was a trap? It is your duty to let your superior know when he would be pushing you too hard, without threatening or warning. And if he does not get the message, then one or both of you are at fault.

And how about this book? Is the book itself disloyal? I think not, but I should say that a book written at the end of an administration, when the job is done, the President has gone into retirement, and the officer has neither quit nor been fired, enjoys a degree of liberty greater than what is owed in medias res, when a former official's words could be used against his chief and colleagues. Still, there is something to make one uneasy about using not actual secrets but confidences, the confidences in which superiors, colleagues, subordinates open themselves to you because the job requires it, or because it offers relief in moments of strain. To turn those occasions against your confidant seems an act of betrayal.[52] But there are other duties—duties to truth and duties to yourself. The public's business should be understandable, transparent, and if those who have been engaged in it are never to give a sense of its texture, of its human feel, we will be left, from administration to administration, from regime to regime, with a mystery and a sham about what it is like to exercise power and to deal with others who have power. That should not be the case in a democracy. Most citizens will never hold office, and they should be let in on the experience.

But that is too lofty an explanation to capture what moves most writers of books like this—what moved me. The public justification I have just offered is a justification, but only that. The real motive is personal. If your book is honest, if it does not seek to excuse you or settle scores, it is a way of making sense of your life. Surely, if you do no harm, this is a right you retain. It is not enough to order your experience privately or for a few friends. The experience was a public one. To be true to that experience, the retrospective must be public too. Office is held by human beings with passions and weaknesses, not just by embodied representatives of abstract programs and concerted interests. Those who have been governed should be able to see this about those who govern them. The official himself should always keep that in mind: humanity, his own and the humanity of others, will always be there. He can try either to banish it or try somehow to embrace and integrate it.

I believe that each of us must try to live the best life he can. Every intense and prolonged experience is a use of the one life we have; it is never lived for others alone, but for itself as well. Too many public men become the role they occupy. Instead of their inhabiting the role, it inhabits them and leaves nothing over. Reflection, analysis, and report reclaim our public lives, if only retrospectively, for our private selves. In this I was lucky. I had been a teacher and a writer, so I had the habit. But I was frightened that it would slip away. The trick I used to reserve a part of myself for myself was to keep a journal, in which I had to account to a private self for what the public self did and felt. This book comes out of that exercise— out of the habit of mind it nurtured, not out of its particular pages, which I have hardly consulted. If I am right that this made me a better public man because not totally a public man, then that is the final justification for this book and any disloyalties it may contain.

NOTES

Introduction: The Reagan Revolution and the Law

[1] F. Bastiat, *Selected Essays on Political Economy*, trans. S. Cain (1964), original in *Journal des Débats*, September 25, 1848.

[2] See, generally, Bloch, "The Early Role of the Attorney General in Our Constitutional Scheme," *Duke Law Journal*, 1989, p. 561.

[3] For an excellent survey of the spectrum of environmental attitudes and groups, see *The New Republic*, April 30, 1990.

[4] Brennan, "The Constitution of the United States: Contemporary Ratification," Federalist Society, 1986, The Great Debate.

[5] Chayes, "The Role of the Judge in Public Law Litigation," *Harvard Law Review*, 89 (1976): p. 1281; but see Fuller, "The Forms and Limits of Adjudication," *Harvard Law Review*, 92 (1978): p. 353. In *Brock* v. *UAW*, 477 U.S. 274 (1986) my Deputy and Counselor, Carolyn Kuhl, launched a frontal attack on this trend, arguing that groups should not have standing to make claim except as they could show themselves to be representatives of classes of individuals in traditional class actions. A vast array of organizations, ranging from the Chamber of Commerce through the AMA to the NAACP, opposed our submission. It was rejected by the Court with no dissent.

[6] *Webster* v. *Reproductive Health Services*, 109 S. Ct. 3040 (1989).

[7] *Bowsher* v. *Synar*, 478 U.S. 714 (1986).

[8] *Morrison* v. *Olson*, 487 U.S. 654 (1988).

[9] *Mistretta* v. *United States*, 488 U.S. 361 (1989).

Chapter 1: Setting the Scene

[1] See, e.g., Fried, *Contract as Promise: A Theory of Contractual Obligation* (1981); "Individual and Collective Rights in Work Relations," *University of Chicago Law Review*, 51 (1984): p. 1012;

"Fast and Loose in the Welfare State," *Regulation,* May-June (1979), p. 13.

[2] *Bowsher* v. *Synar,* 478 U.S. 714 (1986); *Morrison* v. *Olson,* 487 U.S. 654 (1988).

[3] Justin Kaplan, *Walt Whitman: A Life* (1980), p. 273.

[4] Horowitz puts in some quite characteristic cameo appearances in Peggy Noonan's *What I Saw at the Revolution: A Political Life in the Reagan Era* (1990).

[5] Exec. Order No. 11246, establishing Office of Federal Contract Compliance Programs (OFCCP).

[6] *Bob Jones University* v. *United States,* 461 U.S. 574 (1983).

[7] *Chadha* (*INS* v. *Chadha,* 462 U.S. 919 [1983]), which declared unconstitutional the legislative veto found in over two hundred statutes; the Pawtucket crèche case (*Lynch* v. *Donnelly,* 465 U.S. 668 [1984]), holding that a Christmas display in a public park did not violate the Establishment Clause of the First Amendment; *Stotts* (*Firefighters Local Union No. 1784* v. *Stotts,* 467 U.S. 561 [1984]), an important limitation on racial preferences; and *Leon* (*United States* v. *Leon,* 468 U.S. 897 [1984]), which introduced the first major qualification to the rule that illegally seized evidence may not be introduced in a criminal trial.

[8] E.g., *Watt* v. *Community for Creative Non-Violence,* 464 U.S. 812 (1983); *Lynch* v. *Donnelly,* 466 U.S. 994 (1984); *Chevron* v. *Natural Resource Defense Council,* 467 U.S. 837 (1984).

[9] *Jaffree* v. *Board of School Commissioners of Mobile County,* 554 F. Supp. 1104 (S.D. Ala. 1983).

[10] Hand's view of the original conception of the Establishment Clause had eminent historical and scholarly backing. See *Wallace* v. *Jaffree,* 472 U.S. 38, 92 (1985) (Rehnquist, J., dissenting); Fairman, "Does the Fourteenth Amendment Incorporate the Bill of Rights? The Original Understanding," *Stanford Law Review,* 2 (1949): p. 5.

[11] E.g., *Davidson* v. *Cannon,* 474 U.S. 344 (1986); *Solorio* v. *United States,* 483 U.S. 435 (1987); *Webster* v. *Reproductive Services,* 109 S. Ct. 3040 (1989).

[12] I had to resign my professorship at the beginning of 1987, after almost two years in office.

[13] Charles Rule succeeded Douglas Ginsburg as Anti-Trust chief. Roger Marzulla became head of the Lands Division. Chuck Cooper, who was Brad Reynolds' Deputy in Civil Rights, became head of the Office of Legal Counsel, where he enforced strict adherence to principles of federalism and separation of powers.

[14] 476 U.S. 747 (1986).

[15] E.g., Bickel, *The Morality of Consent* (1975), pp. 27–29; Cox, *The Role of the Supreme Court in American Government* (1976), pp. 113–14; Ely, "The Wages of Crying Wolf: A Comment on Roe v. Wade," *Yale Law Journal,* 82 (1973): p. 920; *Democracy and Distrust* (1980), pp. 2–3, 248n.; Freund, "Storms over the Supreme Court," *American Bar Association Journal,* 69 (1983): pp. 1474, 1480; Gunther, "Some Reflections on the Judicial Role: Distinctions, Roots and Prospects," *Washington University Law Quarterly,* 1979, pp. 817, 819; Wellington, "Common Law Rules and Constitutional Double Standards: Some Notes on Adjudication," *Yale Law Journal,* 83 (1973): pp. 221, 297–311.

[16] *City of Akron* v. *Akron Center for Reproductive Health, Inc.,* 462 U.S. 416 (1983).

[17] *Wisconsin* v. *Gould,* 475 U.S. 282 (1986).

[18] *Wygant* v. *Board of Education,* 476 U.S. 267 (1986).

[19] Confirmation Hearings on Federal Appointments, Hearings Before the Committee on the Judiciary, pt. 2, *U.S. Senate, 99th Cong.,* 1st sess., J-99-7, pp. 485–501, October 17, 1985. The only opposition to my nomination came from the NAACP and was based on an incomprehensible but completely mistaken reading of a Gandhian meditation on civil disobedience I had written in 1964 ("Moral Causation," *Harvard Law Review,* 77 [1964]: p. 1258).

[20] 349 U.S. 294 (1955).

[21] 384 U.S. 436 (1966).

[22] 488 U.S. 469 (1989) (racial preferences constitutionally suspect, whether favoring blacks or whites).

[23] The civil-service laws make it illegal to consider political affiliation in filling career posts. See 5 U.S.C. § 3301 (1988); Exec. Order No. 8743 (1941). Nothing is said of philosophical commitments, and I would suppose that the Civil Rights Division in Bobby Kennedy's Justice Department paid as much attention to philosophical commitment as the conservative operatives, following the Heritage Foundation prescriptions, would have had us do now. See, e.g., *Mandate for Leadership, III: Policy Strategies for the 1990's,* ed. Heatherly and Pines (1989).

[24] *Guardians Ass'n* v. *Civil Service Comm'n,* 463 U.S. 582 (1983).

[25] 427 U.S. 160 (1976).

[26] *Edwards* v. *Aguillard,* 482 U.S. 578 (1987).

[27] *Texas* v. *Johnson,* 109 S. Ct. 2533 (1989).

[28] For Meese's public position on *Miranda,* see *The Wall Street Journal,* June 13, 1986, p. 22, col. 4.

[29] ALI, "Model Code of Pre-Arraignment Procedure," council draft no. 1 (1965).

[30] 479 U.S. 157 (1986).

[31] *Colorado* v. *Spring,* 479 U.S. 564 (1987).

[32] *Moran* v. *Burbine,* 475 U.S. 412 (1986).

[33] For a detailed and largely accurate account of this meeting, reported with the assistance of the Department's public-affairs officer, Pat Korten, see *The Legal Times of Washington,* May 4, 1987, p. 2, col. 1.

[34] Office of Professional Responsibility, U.S. Department of Justice, *Results of Our Review of the Independent Counsel's Inquiry into Certain Activities of Attorney General Edwin Meese III* (1988).

[35] Stein, *Report of Independent Counsel in re Edwin Meese, III* (1984).

[36] For instance, on overruling *Miranda,* or on property rights in *First English,* 482 U.S. 304 (1987), where the Court agreed with him and not me, or on overruling *Runyon* v. *McCrary.*

[37] *Federal Bar News and Journal,* 32 (1985): p. 406; *National Law Journal,* September 30, 1985, p. 3.